RE IMAGINING POLICE

THE FUTURE OF PUBLIC SAFETY

REIMAG

INING POLICE

THE FUTURE OF PUBLIC SAFETY

DR. ARTIKA R. TYNER

TWENTY-FIRST CENTURY BOOKS / MINNEAPOLIS

This book is dedicated to my law students at the University of St. Thomas School of Law due to their commitment to building a more just and inclusive society.

Twenty-First Century Books™
An imprint of Lerner Publishing Group, Inc.
241 First Avenue North
Minneapolis, MN 55401 USA

For reading levels and more information, look up this title at
www.lernerbooks.com.

Main body text set in Avenir LT Std.
Typeface provided by Linotype.
Diagrams by Laura K. Westlund, pp. 15, 32, 33, 53, 58, 83, 96.

Library of Congress Cataloging-in-Publication Data

Names: Tyner, Artika R., author.
Title: Reimagining police : the future of public safety / Dr. Artika R. Tyner.
Description: Minneapolis, MN : Lerner Publishing Group, [2023] | Includes
    bibliographical references and index. | Audience: Ages 11–18 | Audience:
    Grades 7–9 | Summary: "Readers will learn about the history of law
    enforcement, approaches to public safety, and strategies for building a
    more just and inclusive society in this survey of policing and reform in
    the United States"— Provided by publisher.
Identifiers: LCCN 2023010712 (print) | LCCN 2023010713 (ebook) |
    ISBN 9781728449630 (library binding) | ISBN 9781728485935 (epub)
Subjects: LCSH: Police—Juvenile literature. | Police—United States—
    Juvenile literature. | CYAC: Law enforcement—United States—Juvenile
    literature. | BISAC: YOUNG ADULT NONFICTION / Law & Crime |
    YOUNG ADULT NONFICTION / Social Topics / Prejudice & Racism
Classification: LCC HV7922 .T96 2023 (print) | LCC HV7922 (ebook) | DDC
    363.2/0973—dc23/eng/20230306

LC record available at https://lccn.loc.gov/2023010712
LC ebook record available at https://lccn.loc.gov/2023010713

Manufactured in the United States of America
1-50433-49942-6/12/2023

CONTENTS

INTRODUCTION
A TIME FOR CHANGE

In the early evening of May 25, 2020, police were called to Cup Foods, a local convenience store in Minneapolis, Minnesota. The store's clerk alleged that an unarmed Black patron, George Floyd, was attempting to use a fake twenty-dollar bill for his purchase. Four officers arrived on the scene and arrested Floyd. Witnesses stated Floyd did not resist arrest. Yet a white officer named Derek Chauvin pinned Floyd to the ground, facedown. He held his knee on Floyd's neck for nearly nine minutes, undeterred by Floyd's repeated statements—twenty-seven of them—that he could not breathe. Nor did Chauvin respond to the pleas of bystanders to let him up. The other three officers, Alexander Kueng, Thomas Lane, and Tou Thao, did not intervene, and Chauvin continued to kneel on Floyd's neck even as he cried out for help from his deceased mother while Kueng knelt on Floyd's back and Lane held his legs. When Floyd became unresponsive, police dispatch called paramedics to the scene while the officers continued to hold Floyd on the ground. An ambulance transported Floyd to a nearby local hospital, where medics pronounced him dead.

On this fateful night, seventeen-year-old Darnella Frazier was walking with her younger cousin, Judeah Reynolds, to Cup Foods. She arrived during Floyd's arrest, joined a crowd of witnesses, pulled out her cell phone, and recorded a video of the deadly encounter between Floyd and the police. Later that day, she posted it to Facebook, where it quickly went viral. Many viewers believed the incident spoke to structural

The intersection outside of Cup Foods in Minneapolis has been turned into a memorial to George Floyd and is considered a space for racial healing and justice.

racism and police brutality experienced by the Black community in the United States. Frazier's videotape sparked national protests and a global movement for racial justice.

The Minneapolis Police Department fired the four officers the day after George Floyd's murder, and they were arrested a few days later. Protests against Floyd's murder ensued across the United States, with tens of thousands of people in more than 140 cities taking to the streets to demand accountability for George Floyd's death. International supporters also organized and mobilized from Brazil to Belgium. Some demonstrators knelt together in town squares, while others remained silent for the nine minutes during which Floyd pled for his life and struggled to breathe. Still, others marched, carrying signs that read "Justice for George Floyd" and chanting "Black Lives Matter." Throughout the summer

Protesters gather in Los Angeles outside of city hall on June 3, 2020. The murder of Floyd sparked protests across the country.

of 2020, the protests transformed into a global movement for advancing policing reform, eradicating racism, and ensuring equal justice under the law.

Chauvin went to trial the next spring. Millions watched the live televised trial, and more than twenty-three million people watched the verdict on April 20, 2021. The jury found Chauvin guilty of second-degree unintentional murder, third-degree murder, and second-degree manslaughter. He was sentenced to twenty-two and half years in prison. A year later, Chauvin filed an appeal to overturn his conviction. Chauvin also had a separate federal case. As part of a plea agreement, Chauvin pleaded guilty in December to federal civil rights charges related to Floyd's death and the restraint of a teenager in a separate incident.

The other three officers, Kueng, Lane, and Thao, were charged with aiding and abetting in the death of Floyd. The officers were also charged in federal court for violating Floyd's rights by not providing medical support and not stopping Chauvin from pressing his knee on Floyd's neck. Kueng was sentenced to three years in prison. Thao was sentenced to three and a half years in prison. Lane pleaded guilty to lesser federal charges related to violating Floyd's civil rights and was sentenced to two and half years in federal prison. The officers also faced state charges. Lane and Kueng entered a plea agreement for a lesser charge and did not stand trial. Lane also pleaded guilty to state charges of aiding and abetting second-degree manslaughter and was sentenced to three

Officer Derek Chauvin (*right, in suit*) is put in handcuffs after being found guilty on April 20, 2021, for the death of George Floyd.

BLACK LIVES MATTER

"It's important for us to also understand that the phrase 'Black Lives Matter' simply refers to the notion that there's a specific vulnerability for African Americans that needs to be addressed. It's not meant to suggest that other lives don't matter. It's to suggest that other folks aren't experiencing this particular vulnerability."

—Barack Obama, forty-fourth president
of the United States

The Black Lives Matter (BLM) movement is a social justice movement that originated in the United States in 2013 in response to the acquittal of George Zimmerman in the killing of Trayvon Martin. The movement seeks to address systemic racism and police brutality against Black people and has organized protests, rallies, and other forms of activism both in the US and globally.

On the other hand, the Black Lives Matter Global Network is a formal organization that was founded in 2016 by a group of activists who were involved in the origins of the BLM movement. Alicia Garza, Patrisse Cullors, and Ayo Tometi founded the Black Lives Matter Global Network with the mission to "eradicate white supremacy and build local power to intervene in violence inflicted on Black communities by the state and vigilantes." The BLM Global Network operates as a decentralized network with local chapters across the United States and around the world.

years in prison. Kueng pleaded guilty to aiding and abetting manslaughter and was sentenced to three and a half years. Thao chose a stipulated trial where the judge makes the final determination of his fate instead of a trial by jury and was found guilty.

For many, Floyd's murder initiated a social justice awakening. For others, he was the latest victim in a long history of police brutality. Together, using demonstrations, community outreach, and political action, they demanded accountability from police departments and the city governments that run them. The movement for accountability sparked intense conversations about policing in the United States and about what public safety should look like in the future.

Reimagining Police

This book examines the intersection of policing and race in the United States. The nation's earliest police forces date back to colonial constables that terrorized Indigenous communities during land removal and displacement. Later, the same pattern of violence and force were used to protect business owners and companies focused on safeguarding economic interests. For example, in northern communities such as Boston, Massachusetts, this meant protecting shipments of goods from the South that passed through the harbor. Often the cargo was enslaved peoples being transported to the South as a part of the slave trade. This meant early police forces played a role in preserving the institution of slavery. In the South, slave patrols monitored the movements of enslaved Black people, capturing those who tried to escape or revolt and returning them to the enslavers' plantations. After the Civil War (1861–1865), these southern patrols transformed into local and state police forces that enforced Black codes and Jim Crow laws. Black codes were enacted starting in 1865 to maintain systems of racial oppression against the recently freed Black community. Jim Crow laws followed as a tool to require racial segregation in such areas as public transportation, schooling, and libraries.

Understanding the history of policing allows us to identify the roots of modern-day harms experienced by communities of color, including structural racism and police brutality. Nearly one thousand Americans are killed each

WHO WAS JIM CROW?

Jim Crow was a fictional character popularized by Thomas Dartmouth Rice, a white actor, in the 1830s. Rice performed in blackface, imitating the mannerisms and speech of enslaved Africans. Rice's Jim Crow character was popular in minstrel shows, which featured songs, dances, and skits that reinforced racist beliefs. The Jim Crow character was portrayed as lazy, unintelligent, and clownlike and perpetuated harmful stereotypes about Black people.

The term "Jim Crow" later became associated with the laws and customs that enforced racial segregation in the southern United States. Jim Crow laws passed in the late nineteenth and early twentieth centuries were based on the idea of "separate but equal." They mandated the segregation of public spaces, including schools, restaurants, public transportation, and housing. These laws also denied Black people the right to vote and restricted their access to education, employment, and other opportunities, and the laws were enforced using violence and intimidation. Black people who challenged the system or attempted to exercise their rights were often subject to harassment, arrest, and aggression. The civil rights movement of the 1950s and 1960s led to the eventual dismantling of the Jim Crow system.

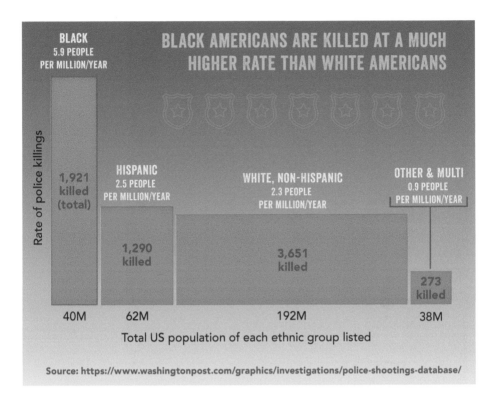

year due to the deadly use of force by police. People of color experience this violence at disproportionally higher rates than white people. Native Americans are killed by police at a rate three times as high, Black Americans more than twice as high, and Hispanic Americans 1.3 times as high as their white counterparts. People of color also experience higher rates of harsh sentencing and tough penalties than white people. Research demonstrates that racial bias can impact outcomes in the justice system, from initial interaction with law enforcement to sentencing.

The goal of public safety is to build and maintain strong and safe communities for everyone. Many people play a role in public safety. Firefighters, emergency medical technicians (EMTs), and police officers fall under this larger umbrella of

DEFINING POLICING

The word *police* emerged from the Greek word *polis* for "city" and *politia* the Latin word for "citizenship." The origins of the word *policing* informs the context of public safety and the role of law enforcement in society. The reference to citizenship focuses on how public safety is rooted in relationships of people and how they work together to solve problems. Policing explores the role of law enforcement in serving the needs of the community with two key goals: protect and serve.

public safety. Community members also play a key role by strengthening their neighborhoods, working to prevent crime, and helping their neighbors when they are in need.

Police officers are supposed to serve in the community and address the needs of people. English philosopher Jeremy Bentham noted that the police keep the peace and that the justice system addresses the penalty of a crime. This is an acknowledgment of the accountability of law enforcement to the people and establishes the role of the judicial system in administering justice when a crime has occurred.

No matter the size of the department, officers must stand ready to meet the needs of the community that they serve in real time. People dial 911 to seek help and support when an emergency arises.

To create a public safety system that works, we must tap into our core values—our shared humanity and common destiny. We must feel a shared responsibility for its success.

This book is not an indictment of police departments, nor is it an anti-police manifesto. Demanding police accountability does not equate to rejecting the police. Reimagining public safety measures requires that police and communities work together toward common goals. The two groups are inextricably interconnected and bound together in the pursuit of a brighter future. This book explores the history of law enforcement and the role of police and community values in protecting public safety. It suggests strategies for building a more just and inclusive society, breaking down proposals for new models of policing and how community members can play a role in developing the blueprints for a more equitable system of public safety. It will provide you with information and tools to lead change in your community.

"The police are the public and . . . the public are the police, the police being only members of the public who are paid to give full-time attention to duties which are incumbent on every citizen in the interests of community welfare and existence."

—Robert Peel

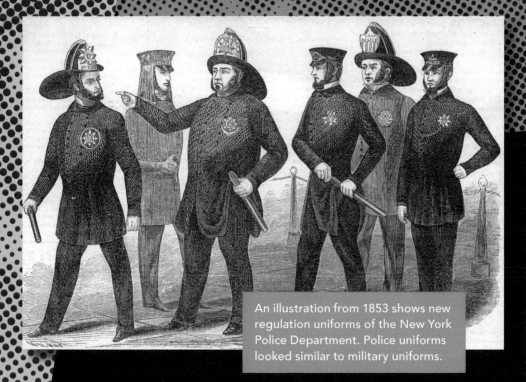

An illustration from 1853 shows new regulation uniforms of the New York Police Department. Police uniforms looked similar to military uniforms.

CHAPTER 1

HISTORY OF POLICING

From early Indigenous practices to slave patrols, different models of public safety and policing have existed. Gaining a deeper understanding of this history can aid in identifying where our present-day issues, such as racial justice, originated. This exploration can help us consider what kinds of changes we can implement to make public safety more effective, inclusive, and equitable.

Some form of policing has been a part of American society since colonial times. Historically, North American Indigenous communities focused on community well-being, care, and community connections as goals, which informed the model of public safety in these communities. These Indigenous public safety models sometimes inspired colonial policing systems being formed, but early policing systems in the colonies were often used to maintain the social and economic order rather than to promote justice and fairness. Additionally, any practices incorporated into colonial policing systems were done without input or consent of those Indigenous communities and without recognition of the value and significance of their traditional systems of justice and governance.

Most colonial towns and cities had volunteers as night watchers along with constables, sheriffs, and marshals. The community volunteers patrolled for potential danger, including fire or crime. To supplement the night watch, colonial communities paid constables to act as daytime law enforcement officials.

Constables were meant to maintain order and protect

This formal portrait depicts a police officer from Saint Joseph, Missouri, in the late 1800s.

the colonial community. This often meant that constables oppressed local Indigenous communities. For example, English settlers forcefully seized Indigenous lands to build farms and towns. As violent conflicts between settlers and Indigenous nations increased, protecting colonists from Indigenous attacks became part of a constable's responsibilities. Some constables, called Indian constables, monitored the day-to-day activities of nearby Indigenous communities and threatened violence to keep them from defending themselves against encroaching settlers. Constables sought to replace Indigenous systems and cultural practices that existed for generations. They used English common law and policing practices. As urbanization grew and major metropolitan cities emerged, some cities began to offer day watch to monitor criminal activity. Early records show that the Saint Louis, Missouri, police force was originally created to protect the white community from Native Americans as the city grew.

CONFEDERATE STATES

The Confederate States, also known as the Confederacy, refers to the eleven Southern states that seceded, or separated, from the United States during the Civil War. These states believed in the preservation of slavery and sought to secede from the United States when Abraham Lincoln, who was opposed to the expansion of slavery into new territories, was elected president in 1860. The Confederate States existed until 1865 when they were defeated in the Civil War and readmitted to the Union.

This illustration of a slave patrol dates to 1863. Enslaved people who escaped slavery were sought out by patrolmen and returned to their enslavers.

Slave Patrols

Slave patrols in the pre-Civil War South were a powerful form of oppressive policing. In 1704 South Carolina created the first official slave patrol in the American colonies. The patrol's main function was to reinforce the power structure of slavery by ensuring that plantation owners remained in control of enslaved Africans, who were their economic engine. The patrols were made up of plantation owners, overseers, and other white men who closely monitored the movement of enslaved people to prevent them from escaping northward to freedom. To prevent revolt, patrols broke up gatherings of enslaved people and searched their living quarters for weapons. These activities were illegal and punishable by law. When patrols interacted with the Black community, they targeted and terrorized them by making them show a "pass" that identified their enslaver

THE KU KLUX KLAN

The Ku Klux Klan (KKK or the Klan) is a white supremacist hate group founded in 1865 after the Civil War by Confederate veterans in Pulaski, Tennessee. The Klan used violence, intimidation, and terror tactics, such as lynchings, arson, and other forms of violence, to maintain white supremacy and suppress Black American political and social progress. The group initially disbanded in 1869 but resurfaced in the early twentieth century, following the release of the film *Birth of a Nation*, which glorified the Klan. Its members adopted white robes, masks, and hoods to conceal their identities while they terrorized Black Americans and white allies who sought to build an egalitarian society. During the civil rights era of the 1950s and 1960s, the Klan became more active, often collaborating with law enforcement officials to target and intimidate civil rights activists. The group still exists as a symbol of white supremacy and racial hatred and serves as a reminder of the ongoing struggle for racial justice and equality.

and restricted their movement. They conducted searches of Black people's homes without permission.

Over the course of 150 years, the slave patrol system was just one of many social forces that institutionalized and normalized racially motivated violence. In 1865, as the Civil War was ending, the US Congress passed the Thirteenth Amendment to the US Constitution. The new amendment abolished chattel slavery and involuntary servitude that allowed people to be legally bought and sold as property by an enslaver. This also ended official slave patrols. But white supremacist vigilante groups such as the Ku Klux Klan violently enforced racial segregation in the former

Confederacy through lynching (public hangings) and other terror tactics. The Ku Klux Klan and other groups worked to ensure that newly freed Black Americans would be disenfranchised and not enjoy basic freedoms and liberties.

Early Police Departments

By the early 1800s, informal community-based policing systems continued with volunteer patrols and some part-time officers. Most cities had added a day watch in addition to a

WHITE SUPREMACY

After the Civil War, white supremacists feared the collective power of the Black community to organize for change and secure their rights. White supremacists believe white people are from a superior race and should control and dominate other racial groups. After the Thirteenth Amendment abolished slavery in 1985, white supremacists used violence as a tool to reinforce their power, such as lynchings to create fear in the hearts and minds of African Americans.

White supremacists also restricted access to the ballot box even after the passage of the Fifteenth Amendment to the Constitution, which Congress passed in 1869 and the states ratified in 1870 to grant Black men the right to vote. Fearing the loss of power if the Black community gained political, social, and economic power, southern white supremacist politicians created restrictive laws and policies—from poll taxes to literacy tests— to make voting impossible for people who could not afford the taxes or who could not read. Enslaved people had been forbidden from learning to read or go to school, so many Black Americans were illiterate.

PEEL'S PRINCIPLES

Robert Peel was the prime minister of the United Kingdom from 1834–1835, and again from 1841–1846. In 1829 he founded and created the Metropolitan Police in London. He helped to shape the principles of community policing and developed a framework for professional police conduct, known as Peel's Nine Principles.

1. The basic mission for which the police exist is to prevent crime and disorder.
2. The ability of the police to perform their duties is dependent upon public approval of police actions.
3. Police must secure the willing cooperation of the public in voluntary observance of the law to be able to secure and maintain the respect of the public.
4. The degree of cooperation of the public that can be secured diminishes proportionately to the necessity of the use of physical force.
5. Police seek and preserve public favor not by catering to the public opinion but by constantly demonstrating absolute impartial service to the law.
6. Police use physical force to the extent necessary to secure observance of the law or to restore order only when the exercise of persuasion, advice, and warning is found to be insufficient.
7. Police, at all times, should maintain a relationship with the public that gives reality to the historic tradition that the police are the public and the public are the police; the police being only members of the public who are paid to give full-time attention to duties which are incumbent on every citizen in the interests of community welfare and existence.
8. Police should always direct their action strictly towards their functions and never appear to usurp the powers of the judiciary.
9. The test of police efficiency is the absence of crime and disorder, not the visible evidence of police action in dealing with it.

night watch. Some even added part-time officers in addition to or instead of the constables. Businesses also hired their own private security and protection services to prevent theft of goods. This system of policing was influenced by policing in England, where private citizens oversaw and regulated the safety of their communities.

The Political and Professional Eras

The late 1800s and early 1900s marked what is known as the Political Era of policing in the US. Although many major cities had established formal police forces, a lot of crime still went unchecked. Part of this was because the districts that police departments served corresponded to political wards. The leaders of these wards had a lot of power. They picked police captains and sergeants in their districts. Ward leaders also often ran street gangs or businesses such as bars. They sometimes bribed officers to ignore crimes such as illegal drinking and gambling.

The police were not held in high regard. They were known for having little training or education, taking bribes, and beating people who had been arrested. Organized crime was on the rise, and laws were poorly enforced. Many people considered the police corrupt.

Known as the father of modern policing, August Vollmer helped change the structure and public perception of police. He became a police chief in Berkeley, California, in the early 1900s. While he did not invent many new systems, he was good at building on existing ideas, and he embraced new technologies. Vollmer instituted bike and car patrols, encouraged radio use in squad cars, and supported fingerprinting technology. John Larson, a PhD student at University of California, Berkeley, created the first lie detector test in 1921 at Vollmer's request. The next year Vollmer became the Los Angeles Police Department chief and began hot spots policing. Under this patrol model, police identify neighborhoods with higher crime rates and place officers on the streets there.

Vollmer changed the internal structure of the police too. He helped create police training programs and even recruited officers directly from universities. Police began to wear uniforms and were organized in ranks. The idea of having a career as a cop was born.

August Vollmer became Berkeley's first chief of police in 1909.

Most of Vollmer's ideas and tactics were inspired by his time in the military. They were an early form of militarization. Militarization incorporates military tactics and equipment into police models. From patrol models to uniforms, his tactics are still common in modern American policing.

Volmer's efforts helped end the Political Era of policing and begin the Professional Era. The Political Era found its end with the 1929 launch of a presidential commission created to enforce laws and cut back on organized crime. Soon after, the map of police districts was changed to no longer match political wards.

The Start of Federal Police

Vollmer's tactics spread nationwide throughout the early 1900s. But even as local and state policing improved, federal security agents had little power. In 1924 J. Edgar Hoover became the director of the Bureau of Investigation (BOI), later renamed Federal Bureau of Investigation (FBI). At the time, BOI agents reported to state police. They couldn't make arrests or carry weapons unless they were also deputies with a local police force. Many US citizens also didn't support a national police force. They feared it would become a secret police force or have too much power.

Hoover led a campaign to gain public trust throughout the 1930s. As Vollmer did with state police, Hoover helped professionalize federal security by emphasizing education and encouraging the use of advanced police skills alongside scientific methods. He insisted federal agents have training in forensic sciences and the use of firearms and have strong qualifications such as college degrees. Hoover also expanded the agency's fingerprint files into the largest collection available with over six million fingerprints stored.

The BOI briefly became the Division of Investigation in 1933. The next year President Franklin D. Roosevelt signed a bill granting the federal government more power by letting federal agents carry firearms and make arrests. The force became the Federal Bureau of Investigation in 1935 and is still the main national security organization in the US.

Equal Rights Movements Respond to Police Violence

Public favor of state and federal law enforcement had grown by the middle of the twentieth century, but both still had problems. Only white men could become special agents in the FBI—neither white women nor any people of color could. The state police were growing more militarized, and police violence spiked.

Many communities protested police brutality. One of the aims of the civil rights movement of the 1950s and 1960s was to challenge discrimination such as racial profiling and police brutality against Black people. Civil rights activists suggested ways to curb discrimination, including hiring more Black officers and involving civilians in overseeing police through the establishment of civilian review boards. Others advocated for accessing better training and fostering community engagement.

The civil rights movement and the other movements of the time did not end police violence. But they marked a historic point when people came together to protest and voice ways to reform the structure of police.

New York police officers are inspected by the chief before going on duty in 1950. Police forces were primarily made up of all-white, all-male members.

THE STONEWALL RIOTS

Police violence also affects other marginalized groups. In the 1960s, LGBTQ+ acts were illegal everywhere except Illinois, and police frequently raided LGBTQ+ businesses across the US. It came to a head in June 1969 when police arrested several employees and seized illegal alcohol from Stonewall Inn, an LGBTQ+ bar in New York City. During a second raid a few days later, they arrested more employees and customers. Two trans women of color, Marsha P. Johnson and Sylvia Rivera, resisted arrest. Other people joined, and the Stonewall riots began.

Police beat and used tear gas against many people at the riots. But Stonewall supporters continued to protest police raids and discrimination against LGBTQ+ people all weekend. The riots ended after a few days, but the LGBTQ+ rights movement grew quickly in their wake. A year later, the first New York City Pride event was held and capped off with a march beginning at Stonewall Inn.

The War on Drugs

Changes in criminal law in the twentieth century had a significant impact on the criminal justice system. In 1971 US president Richard Nixon declared a "War on Drugs," calling drug misuse "public enemy number one" and focusing his policy-making efforts on combating drug trafficking. During his presidency from 1981–1989, Ronald Reagan expanded these policies to address the impact of drugs on American society such as higher rates of drug use and the potential increase in criminal behavior.

In 1980 the number of people incarcerated for drug-related offenses of sales and distribution was 50,000. It was 430,926 by 2019. A key contributing factor to this large increase in incarceration rates was a change in how society sought to address drug use. Historically, drug crimes had been addressed through rehabilitation, following a model that viewed drug abuse as a health issue. This prioritized treatment and health services instead of criminalizing drug use. But under Reagan, the federal government adopted a more punitive approach. Reagan signed the Anti-Drug Abuse Act in 1986, which allocated $1.7 billion for drug enforcement. Under this new law, penalties for drug crimes were intensified by implementing mandatory minimums on drug-related offenses. This required a sentence for a drug crime to be at a predetermined number of years set by law. This left judges without discretion to decide a sentence based on the facts. This lack of discretion prevented judges from reducing a sentence in the hope of supporting an offender's rehabilitation or using a diversion program, an alternative to incarceration. They had to follow specific sentencing guidelines. The tough-on-crime approach meant that people would face harsher penalties for nonviolent drug offenses than they had in previous decades. Many drug charges were reclassified from low-level misdemeanor offenses, which carried a shorter prison sentence to felony offenses. Felony offenses had harsher penalties such as more years in prison and imposed collateral consequences.

In the 1980s, law enforcement practices also changed. Police units became even more militarized to enforce the new Reagan-era drug policies. Special Weapons and Tactics (SWAT) teams, first developed in the 1960s, were made up of officers specially trained to deal with highly dangerous situations. And military-grade weapons provided by the US government became increasingly common within local

Nancy Reagan speaks at the first National Federation of Parents for Drug-Free Youth conference in 1982. Reagan focused much of her efforts as First Lady on her Just Say No campaign to encourage kids to "just say no" to drugs.

police forces. The continued militarization of local police forces left many communities feeling as if they were in an occupied state or war zone because the uniforms and protective gear, in addition to their assault rifles, looked similar to the military.

Stricter drug enforcement and increased police presence on the streets continued into the 1990s under the Clinton administration (1993–2001). In 1994 Bill Clinton signed a new federal crime bill called the Violent Crime Control and Law Enforcement Act. It included grant funding to add one hundred thousand new police officers across the United States. The act also increased the length of mandatory prison sentences for drug-related offenses and allocated additional funds to build more prisons and jails.

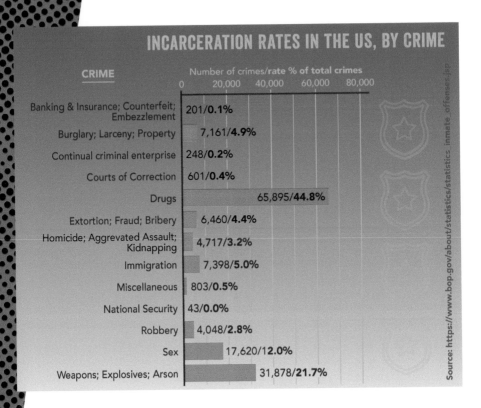

INCARCERATION RATES IN THE US, BY CRIME

CRIME	Number of crimes/rate % of total crimes
Banking & Insurance; Counterfeit; Embezzlement	201/0.1%
Burglary; Larceny; Property	7,161/4.9%
Continual criminal enterprise	248/0.2%
Courts of Correction	601/0.4%
Drugs	65,895/44.8%
Extortion; Fraud; Bribery	6,460/4.4%
Homicide; Aggrevated Assault; Kidnapping	4,717/3.2%
Immigration	7,398/5.0%
Miscellaneous	803/0.5%
National Security	43/0.0%
Robbery	4,048/2.8%
Sex	17,620/12.0%
Weapons; Explosives; Arson	31,878/21.7%

Source: https://www.bop.gov/about/statistics/statistics_inmate_offenses.jsp

The United States, home to only 5 percent of the world's population, incarcerates over 20 percent of the world's prison population. Nearly two million people are in prison or jail in the United States. Another 3.9 million are on probation or parole. The term *mass incarceration* is used to refer to this systemic challenge that combines the criminal justice, penal (corrections), and policing systems. Mass incarceration disproportionately affects Black communities and other communities of color. Because of this, it is sometimes called the New Jim Crow.

Modern Police Departments

The United States has over eighteen thousand local and state police departments. They serve large metropolitan

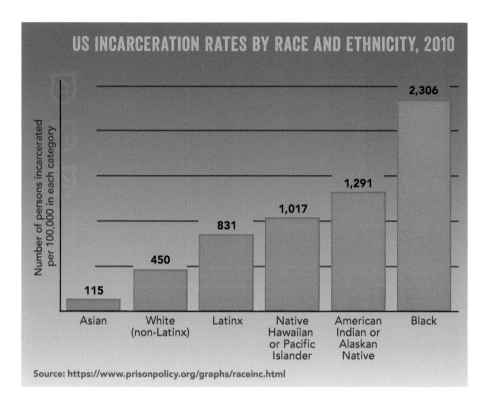

US INCARCERATION RATES BY RACE AND ETHNICITY, 2010

Number of persons incarcerated per 100,000 in each category

| Asian | White (non-Latinx) | Latinx | Native Hawaiian or Pacific Islander | American Indian or Alaskan Native | Black |

115 450 831 1,017 1,291 2,306

Source: https://www.prisonpolicy.org/graphs/raceinc.html

cities as well as smaller rural communities. Some departments are very large—New York City has thirty-six thousand police officers—but most departments have fewer than fifty officers. Modern police departments are responsible for a large number of public safety duties. They keep people safe by preventing and addressing criminal activity, responding to medical and mental health emergencies, de-escalating and resolving disputes between civilians, managing traffic flow, enforcing parking rules, solving crimes as detectives, and helping those in need to find food and shelter. They also walk the streets as beat cops to help build community connections. This type of high visibility in patrolling can aid in deterring crime in a neighborhood. According to the 2018 Department of Justice

THE OATH AND BADGE

A police officer takes an oath of honor when graduating from the police academy. The oath is a promise to uphold principles of justice, integrity, and fairness. The following is the general oath:

On my honor, I will never betray my integrity, my character, or the public trust. I will treat all individuals with dignity and respect and ensure that my actions are dedicated to ensuring the safety of my community and the preservation of human life. I will always have the courage to hold myself and others accountable for our actions. I will always maintain the highest ethical standards and uphold the values of my community, and the agency I serve.

The oath is taken before earning one's badge. The badge represents authority, purpose, and responsibility. It identifies a police officer as a problem solver and protector. The police badge is worn on the left side over the heart as a reminder to protect and honor the community served.

State police wearing military-style gear gather as part of a SWAT team response during a lockdown at Yale University in New Haven, Connecticut, in 2013. Police received a report someone was seen carrying a gun on campus.

data, police officers had interactions with approximately 61.5 million people within a year while fulfilling these duties. Police officers make about ten million arrests a year. Most encounters with the police never make headline news and do not result in an arrest.

New York City police officers stand in front of their police station in the 1880s.

CHAPTER 2

RACE AND POLICING

Some communities, especially communities of color, may fear or distrust the police. They may understand policing as a mechanism to control a community and uphold white supremacy. This view of policing is based on historical and modern-day encounters between police and people of color.

Institutional Racism: From Slave Patrols to Jim Crow

The Civil War came to an end on April 9, 1865, with the South losing the war. Following the end of the war, the

Thirteenth Amendment was enacted and Reconstruction was implemented. The Thirteenth Amendment, ratified on December 6, 1865, abolished slavery, but it included an exception clause that read "except as a punishment for crime whereof the party shall have been duly convicted." This meant that convicted prisoners could still be forced to complete unpaid labor. Reconstruction focused on racial equity and justice and aimed to address the economic, social, and political barriers experienced by the Black community due to slavery. It was an opportunity to move Black people from second-class citizenship to full citizenship by enabling them to seek employment, serve in public office, and vote.

During the Reconstruction period (1865–1877), southern lawmakers worked to maintain the prewar racial hierarchy. They instituted restrictive laws controlling the labor and activity of newly freed Black Americans. These Black codes made it illegal for a Black person to be unemployed or to be disrespectful to white people. This meant Black people could be arrested for asking for higher wages or time off, refusing to sign a work contract, or failing to tip their hat to a white person. Once convicted of violating a Black code, a person could be sent out on a convict lease and forced to labor for free. These codes were enforced by all-white police and state militia forces—direct descendants of prewar slave patrols. A militia is an armed group who operate like a police force to uphold their power structures such as white supremacy.

Following Reconstruction, Jim Crow laws in the North and South replaced the Black codes. Jim Crow legalized racial segregation for almost one hundred years leading into the 1960s. These laws restricted equal access to restaurants, public transportation, schools, and other public spaces such as libraries and community pools. Those who challenged

A photo taken in 1940 shows a café in Durham, North Carolina, with separate entrances for white and colored people. Jim Crow laws made this type of segregation legal throughout the country.

segregation laws faced violence from police and vigilantes alike. They were threatened and beaten, and some were killed for questioning the status quo of Jim Crow. More than forty-four hundred racial lynchings occurred from Reconstruction to World War II (1939–1945).

Despite what felt like insurmountable challenges, Black people were determined to be free from racism and oppression. They came together and built their own thriving communities, established their own local governments, and created their own Black businesses. In 1887 Eatonville, Florida, became one of the first Black US towns or municipalities established by formerly enslaved Black Americans. Anthropologist and author Zora Neale Hurston grew up in Eatonville. In 1887 Isaiah T. Montgomery and his cousin Benjamin T. Green, two visionary leaders who had been freed from slavery, founded Mound Bayou, in the Mississippi delta. They bought 840 acres (340 ha) of swampland and transformed it into a Black oasis. The community built a hospital, bank, library, and many successful businesses.

The Greenwood District of Tulsa, Oklahoma, was another Black-owned and established city with a growing economy. The success of its residents and businesses earned it the name Black Wall Street. But that changed during the summer of 1921. A Black male teenager entered an elevator, and at some point, the white female elevator operator let out a scream. The teenager fled for his safety and was later arrested. A white mob gathered in front of the courthouse demanding that he be released to them. The Black community feared that he would be brutalized and lynched. A group of Black men, who were mostly World War I veterans, decided to intervene, seeking to protect the teenager. The white mob grew, and chaos erupted. Public officials deputized the white mob, which meant they were given firearms and ammunition. The mob burned the Black community's homes and businesses. During eighteen hours from May 31 to June 1, 1921, thirty-five blocks were destroyed. This impacted 190 businesses and left ten thousand people without homes. It also claimed at least three hundred lives (the exact number of people killed is still unknown). Hours after the Tulsa massacre, the police concluded that the teenager had merely stumbled or possibly stepped on the white woman's foot. The charges against him were dismissed.

Malcolm X

Malcolm X was a civil rights activist and minister who played a significant role in advocating for the rights of Black Americans. He served as the post minister of Nation of Islam

"The common goal of 22 million Afro-Americans is respect as human beings, the God-given right to be a human being. Our common goal is to obtain the human rights that America has been denying us. We can never get civil rights in America until our human rights are first restored. We will never be recognized as citizens there until we are first recognized as humans."

—*Malcolm X*

Temple No. 7 Mosque in Harlem. In 1957 Malcolm X publicly spoke out against police brutality there after a member of the Nation of Islam, Johnson Hinton, and two other Black men intervened as the police assaulted a young Black man, Reece Poe. The police then severely beat Hinton, arrested all the men, and brought them to the police department.

Malcolm X heard about the arrest from a witness, went to the police station, and demanded to see Hinton. He was denied at first, but a crowd formed to protest, and Malcom X was finally allowed to see Hinton, who was covered in blood and semiconscious. He demanded medical treatment for Hinton. As the ambulance transported Hinton to the hospital, Malcolm X and the crowd of protesters followed the emergency vehicle fifteen blocks to the hospital. Once Hinton's medical needs were met, Malcolm X dispersed the huge crowd with a wave of his hand.

Malcolm X sued the New York City Police Department and won a settlement in connection with the incident. His advocacy against police brutality and racial injustice gained national attention and contributed to the broader civil rights movement of the era.

The Civil Rights Movement and Nonviolent Protest

During the civil rights movement, US citizens participated in marches, sit-ins, and boycotts for equal rights. Police often met these nonviolent acts of protest with violence. Police beat some demonstrators with batons, while police dogs bit others. Police regularly arrested protesters, both Black and white, for violating segregation laws.

One particularly influential civil rights march occurred on May 2, 1963. That day more than one thousand Black students between the ages of seven and eighteen participated in a mass march in Birmingham, Alabama. The goal of the Children's March, as it was later called, was to draw attention to the harsh realities of racial segregation and the constant threat of violence from police and white supremacist vigilante

Young Black protesters march in Birmingham, Alabama, in May 1963. They called for equal treatments of Blacks in America and an end to racial violence.

Protesters carry signs demanding equal rights as they march on August 28, 1963. During the March on Washington for Jobs and Freedom, or simply the March on Washington, an estimated 250,000 protesters came to Washington, DC, to call for an end to racism.

groups such as the Ku Klux Klan. As the group began to march, the Birmingham police surrounded the peaceful protesters and blocked their path. Police arrested many of the children and detained them in jail. Hundreds more gathered the next day to continue the march. This time, the city's commissioner of public safety, Bull Connor, with the help of Alabama governor George Wallace authorized law enforcement to use force to stop the protesters. Officers clubbed the children, blasted them with high-powered water hoses, and attacked them with police dogs. Americans watched in horror as national television news programs and print press featured images of police hosing down and beating children.

INSPIRING THE COMMUNITY TO LEAD CHANGE

Martin Luther King Jr. was a key leader of the American nonviolent resistance movement during the civil rights movement. His vision was shaped by the ministry of Jesus Christ, who preached love and justice. King also embraced Mohandas Gandhi's teachings of peaceful resistance to oppression. Gandhi, an Indian revolutionary who campaigned for nonviolent civil disobedience, based his thinking on the ancient Hindu philosophy of satyagraha, meaning "holding onto truth."

King outlined six principles of nonviolence:

1. Nonviolence is a way of life for courageous people. It is active nonviolent resistance to evil.
2. Nonviolence seeks to win friendship and understanding. The end result of nonviolence is redemption and reconciliation.
3. Nonviolence seeks to defeat injustice, not people. Nonviolence recognizes that evildoers are also victims.
4. Nonviolence holds that suffering can educate and transform. Nonviolence willingly accepts the consequences to its acts.
5. Nonviolence chooses love instead of hate. Nonviolence resists violence to the spirit as well as the body. Nonviolence love is active, not passive. Nonviolence love does not sink to the level of the hater. Love restores community and resists injustice. Nonviolence recognizes the fact that all life is interrelated.
6. Nonviolence believes that the universe is on the side of justice. The nonviolent resister has deep faith that justice will eventually win.

The violence in Birmingham did not stop protesters. Nor did the police stop using brutal tactics and excessive force to stop protesters. Civil rights organizers led a march for Black voting rights that would travel 54 miles (87 km) from Selma, Alabama, to the state capitol in Montgomery. On Sunday, March 7, 1965, six hundred protesters attempted to cross the Edmund Pettus Bridge, named after a Confederate general who later became a leader in the Ku Klux Klan. But a barricade of armed state troopers and county sheriff deputies met the group—led by Hosea Williams and John Lewis—as they crossed. White community members also gathered, holding Confederate flags. Police beat protesters as they attempted to walk down the sidewalk and across the bridge. Sixteen people were hospitalized, and another

State troopers launched tear gas as marchers neared the end of the Edmund Pettus Bridge in Selma, Alabama, in March 1965.

fifty people were injured. John Lewis, who later became a longtime member of Congress, sustained a skull fracture from a violent beating. That evening nearly fifty million Americans watched news footage of what would later become known as Bloody Sunday.

The Children's March and Bloody Sunday are just two of the many instances of police brutality Black Americans faced as they protested for civil rights. Persistent national coverage of these events placed pressure on the US Congress to pass the Civil Rights Act of 1964. The act guaranteed protection against discrimination on the basis of race, color, religion, sex, or national origin. President Lyndon B. Johnson signed it on July 2, 1964. He signed the Voting Rights Act of 1965 into law as well. While these were major victories for the movement, Black Americans and other communities of color continued to face racial violence by the police.

In many communities, police harassed and intimidated people of color who sought to improve their economic and social standing. Many white Americans in the North believed racial injustice and police brutality existed only in the South. They thought racial injustice was linked to leaders such as Connor and Wallace using their power to maintain the racial hierarchy of segregation. But King argued that racism was a national issue and that to address it, the federal government would have to intervene. King knew that the safety and well-being of Black Americans were threatened no matter where they lived.

The Black Panthers and Policing the Police

College students Huey Newton and Bobby Seale founded the Black Panther Party in Oakland, California, in October 1966. They initially established the organization to combat

THE VOTING RIGHTS ACT

The Voting Rights Act addressed the widespread and systematic disenfranchisement of Black Americans in the southern states, where discriminatory voting practices such as poll taxes, literacy tests, and intimidation had been used to prevent them from exercising their right to vote. The act is regarded as a significant achievement of the civil rights movement, and it has played a crucial role in advancing voting rights for minorities in the United States. It empowered the federal government to oversee and enforce voting rights in areas with a history of discrimination, and it authorized the US Department of Justice to challenge discriminatory practices and changes to voting laws. The Voting Rights Act has been amended several times since its passage, including in 1970, 1975, 1982, and again in 2006, when the coverage formula was updated and extended for another twenty-five years. In 2013 the US Supreme Court decision on *Shelby County v. Holder* meant states with a history of suppressing voting rights would no longer have to submit changes in voting policies to the US Justice Department for review.

police brutality against Black Americans. At the time, the Oakland Police Department was 96 percent white while the city's population was only just over 50 percent white. Many members of the police force were former members of the military and moved to California from a southern state. During the 1960s the Black community faced the mounting challenges of poverty, homelessness, and unemployment. At least one-half of Black Americans were living in poverty and experiencing unemployment at a rate higher than the national average. This created tensions and discontent. Further, police officers followed a law-and-order approach in communities of color, which increased the rate of violence.

In light of this pattern of police violence, one of the core functions of the Black Panthers was to "police the police." In California a person could legally carry a loaded gun as long as it was carried openly. Armed Panthers would monitor police interactions with Black civilians to ensure that no one was brutalized and that the laws that defined proper police behavior were followed. This cop-watching effort was one part of the party's larger mission to support the Black community and defend civil rights. The Black Panthers also helped with community organizing and providing aid.

Founders of the Black Panther Party, Bobby Seale (*left*) and Huey Newton (*right*), sit at party headquarters in San Francisco in 1967.

They established several chapters across the country. These chapters created social programs, such as free breakfasts for schoolchildren and free health clinics, which helped to build solidarity within Black communities.

The Black Panthers saw solidarity as the key to overcoming racial discrimination. Fred Hampton, the Panthers' Illinois chapter chair, said, "Some people say you fight fire best with fire, but we say you put fire out best with water. We say you don't fight racism with racism. We're gonna fight racism with solidarity." Twenty-one-year-old Hampton was murdered by the police on December 4, 1969, in an apartment as he lay asleep. The police alleged that they were attacked while bringing a search warrant for illegal weapons. Over ninety bullets were fired, claiming the lives of Hampton and Mark Clark, another member of the Black Panthers, and critically wounding others in the apartment. FBI

LAW AND ORDER

A law-and-order approach emphasizes strict enforcement of laws and harsh penalties for those who break them. It places an emphasis on maintaining public order, often through aggressive tactics and a "tough on crime" mentality. This approach views crime as an individual choice and focuses on punishing offenders rather than addressing the underlying social and economic factors that contribute to crime. Law-and-order policing often involves a heavy police presence in communities and an emphasis on aggressive tactics such as stop and frisk and broken windows policing. Supporters of this approach argue that it is necessary to maintain public safety and deter crime, while critics argue that it can lead to excessive use of force, racial profiling, and violations of civil liberties.

records later showed a different account of what had happened. The attack was targeted against the Black Panthers to dismantle their organization and ensure a powerful Black leader would not mobilize and take action against the injustices experienced by the Black community.

The Kerner Commission

The importance of addressing racial injustice nationwide came to a head in the late 1960s. Communities of color facing unemployment and inadequate housing took to the streets in cities across the United States to protest injustice, including abusive policing. Rioting broke out in several cities.

The Watts riots in 1965 were a precursor to the "long, hot summer of 1967," In Watts of Los Angeles, California, violence erupted after a twenty-one-year-old Black male, Marquette Frye, was pulled over for reckless driving. The situation escalated, Frye was arrested with force, and the resulting unrest lasted for six days. Martial law was enforced, giving the military temporary authority to take over. "The chaos that ensued left 34 people dead, including 23 killed by Los Angeles Police Department (LAPD) officers or National Guard troops, as well as 1,032 injured, at least 600 buildings damaged from fires or looting, another 200 buildings completely destroyed, and around 3,500 people arrested," *Time* magazine reported. There was an estimated $40 million in property damage. The televised coverage of the uprising drew national attention.

During the summer of 1967, a number of riots broke out sparked by a combination of factors, including long-standing racial tensions, high unemployment rates, poor living conditions in inner cities, and a sense of frustration and anger among Black Americans over ongoing discrimination and police brutality. A riot on July 23 in Detroit, Michigan, saw forty-three people dead, several hundred injured, and more than seven thousand arrested. In response to the historic violence and unrest, President Johnson created a panel of eleven professionals to identify the root causes of the violence. Named after its chair, Illinois governor Otto Kerner Jr., the Kerner Commission explored three key questions: "What happened? Why did it happen? And what can be done to prevent it from happening again and again?"

The commission traveled from city to city searching for answers. They interviewed youth, adults, and government officials to gain insights into the root causes of racial violence. The commission's final 426-page report concluded that systemic racism had limited economic opportunities for Black and Latino Americans. Its most well-known critique stated that the United States was "moving toward two societies, one black, one white—separate and unequal. . . . Discrimination and segregation have long permeated much of American life; they now threaten the future of every American."

The Kerner Commission recommended major financial investments in social welfare, housing, employment, and educational opportunities for communities of color. The goal was to promote racial equity by removing the roadblocks to success that hampered those communities. The report also outlined strategies for improving police and community relations. The commission stressed the importance of addressing police misconduct such as physical abuse, harassment, and unwarranted stops and searches, and providing resources for citizens to express their grievances or complaints about interactions with the police. The commission also emphasized the importance of equity and inclusion. They suggested hiring additional

KEY CHALLENGES IDENTIFIED BY THE KERNER REPORT

Based on survey research and interviews, the commission identified key challenges. They ranked the twelve areas by the intensity of the issue.

FIRST LEVEL OF INTENSITY

1. Police practices
2. Unemployment and underemployment
3. Inadequate housing

SECOND LEVEL OF INTENSITY

1. Inadequate education
2. Poor recreation facilities and programs
3. Ineffectiveness of the political structure and grievance mechanisms.

THIRD LEVEL OF INTENSITY

1. Disrespectful white attitudes
2. Discriminatory administration of justice
3. Inadequacy of federal programs
4. Inadequacy of municipal services
5. Discriminatory consumer and credit practices
6. Inadequate welfare programs

Black officers and investing in more community relations efforts. Instead of taking these recommendations, American politics became more conservative with a tough-on-crime approach. Law-and-order politics increased the pace of police militarization, and the War on Drugs fueled the beginnings of mass incarceration.

Mass Incarceration

Police arrest Black Americans at higher rates than white Americans, and Black Americans are incarcerated at higher rates and for longer terms than white Americans. The disproportionate rate of incarceration of Black Americans has led to a widespread number of individuals experiencing a civil disability from a criminal conviction, such as job prospects and wealth creation possibilities being limited. These challenges begin early in life for Black American youth, who "accounted for 15% of all U.S. children yet made up 35% of juvenile arrests in [2016]." This trend continues into adulthood. In 2016 Black Americans made up 27 percent of all individuals arrested in the United States, double their representation within the general population.

CRIMINAL CONVICTIONS AND COLLATERAL CONSEQUENCES

People who have been convicted of a crime may face restrictions to employment, housing, voting, or education opportunities as part of their sentencing. These barriers are known as collateral consequences. The National Inventory of Collateral Consequences of Conviction created by the American Bar Association includes more than forty thousand collateral consequences. Some restrictions are designed to improve public safety, such as prohibiting people convicted of assault or abuse from working with children or the elderly. But there is often no relationship between the crime and the collateral consequence. A felony conviction can prevent someone from voting in some states such as Alabama.

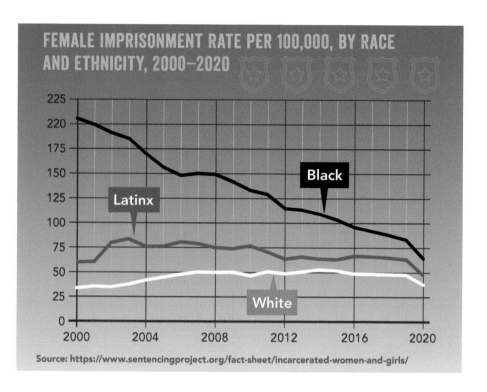

FEMALE IMPRISONMENT RATE PER 100,000, BY RACE AND ETHNICITY, 2000–2020

Black

Latinx

White

225
220
175
150
125
100
75
50
25
0

2000   2004   2008   2012   2016   2020

Source: https://www.sentencingproject.org/fact-sheet/incarcerated-women-and-girls/

According to the US Bureau of Justice Statistics, "African-American adults are 5.9 times as likely to be incarcerated than whites and Hispanics are 3.1 times as likely." Recent trends show a sharp increase in the number of women incarcerated with the number of incarcerated women increasing from 26,378 in 1980 to 152,854 in 2020. Black women are incarcerated at twice the rate of white women.

One of the traumas of mass incarceration is the negative impact on families. Over five million children have or have had an incarcerated parent. Rutgers University's National Resource Center for Children and Families of the Incarcerated cites that one in nine Black children (11.4 percent), one in twenty-eight Hispanic children (3.5 percent), and one in fifty-seven white children (1.8 percent) have an incarcerated parent. Children of incarcerated parents are six times more likely to go to

PERCENTAGE OF CHILDREN WITH INCARCERATED PARENTS BY RACE AND ETHNICITY

Race	Data Type	2018–2019	2019–2020	2020–2021
American Indian	Number	52,823	44,018	48,794
	Percent	20%	16%	18%
Asian and Pacific Islander	Number	34,963	20,771	29,109
	Percent	1%	1%	1%
Black or African American	Number	1,269,509	1,201,057	1,003,666
	Percent	13%	12%	10%
Hispanic or Latino	Number	1,157,507	1,001,877	975,661
	Percent	6%	5%	5%
Non-Hispanic White	Number	2,298,204	2,169,643	2,014,537
	Percent	6%	6%	6%
Total	Number	5,276,031	4,876,252	4,463,973
	Percent	7%	7%	6%

Source: https://datacenter.kidscount.org/data/tables/9734-children-who-had-a-parent-who-was-ever-incarcerated-by-race-and-ethnicity#detailed/1/any/false/1696,1648,1603/10,11,9,12,1,13/18995,18996

prison during their lifetime than children who have not had an incarcerated parent. This relationship creates a ripple effect, passing from one generation to another, thereby increasing the likelihood of a child committing a crime.

According to the Sentencing Project, a criminal justice reform organization, "More than one in four people arrested for drug law violations in 2015 was [B]lack, although drug use rates do not differ substantially by race and ethnicity and drug users generally purchase drugs from people of the same race or ethnicity. For example, the ACLU [American Civil Liberties Union, an organization that focuses on protecting the constitutional rights of everyday people] found that [Black people] were 3.7 times more likely to be arrested for marijuana possession than [white people] in 2010, even though their rate of marijuana usage was comparable."

In another example, during the 1980s, the sentencing ratio of people arrested for possession of crack cocaine versus powder cocaine was a ratio of one hundred to one. Sentencing guidelines treated 5 grams (0.2 ounces) of crack cocaine (about the same amount as five sugar packs) the same as possessing 500 grams (18 ounces) of powder cocaine (about the same size as a loaf of bread). In both instances, the defendant would be sentenced to a mandatory minimum of five years in prison. Yet scientists have not identified any pharmaceutical differences between crack cocaine and powder cocaine.

This sentencing policy appeared neutral at face value. But the ratio had a negative impact on Black communities since Black offenders tended to be arrested more frequently for crack cocaine charges. This inequality ignored that white people frequently use crack and have a similar rate of drug use despite the myth that Black Americans use drugs at a higher rate.

From the Past to the Present

Some people may argue that racism in policing has ended. Only 63 percent of white people believe Black people were treated less favorably by the police than white people, while 84 percent of Black Americans agree. Members of the Black community are five times more likely than the white community to state that they have been treated unfairly by the police.

Recent data suggest that excessive force and police brutality continue to disproportionately impact Black, Indigenous, and other communities of color. In 2021 Black Americans made up 13 percent of the US population. Yet Black people accounted for 27 percent of individuals fatally shot by police.

TAKING A STAND BY TAKING A KNEE

Colin Kaepernick was a talented and promising quarterback with the San Francisco 49ers from 2011 to 2017. At the start of the 2016 National Football League (NFL) season, he made a decision that would alter his career path and incite a national dialogue about racial tensions. He decided he would not stand when the national anthem was played before the game. He sat for the first three preseason games. After a discussion with former NFL player and military veteran Nate Boyer, he decided to kneel for the remainder of the season as a more respectful form of protest.

The move came after a year of high-profile police brutality cases against Black men across the country. On December 2, 2015, twenty-six-year-old Mario Woods was shot over twenty

Colin Kaepernick (*right*) is joined by Eric Reid as they take a knee during the national anthem prior to an NFL football game in September 2016.

times by five officers in San Francisco. Alton Sterling was shot and killed by officers in Baton Rouge, Louisiana, on July 5, 2016. The next day police shot Philando Castile during a traffic stop in Falcon Heights, Minnesota.

Kaepernick wanted to bring attention to the racial injustices experienced by the Black community by the police. "I am not going to stand up to show pride in a flag for a country that oppresses Black people and people of color," Kaepernick explained during an interview. "To me, this is bigger than football and it would be selfish on my part to look the other way. There are bodies in the street and people getting paid leave and getting away with murder."

Some supported his right to protest, including some other players in the league, but he also received strong criticism from NFL fans and owners. Former president Donald Trump encouraged owners to release players who knelt during the anthem. Kaepernick was released at the end of the season, and he was not signed to another team. After leaving the NFL, he continued to advocate against police brutality and serve as a champion for equal rights.

Kaepernick created the Know Your Rights Camp. This youth program for Black and other children of color teaches kids about their legal rights and helps them develop leadership skills.

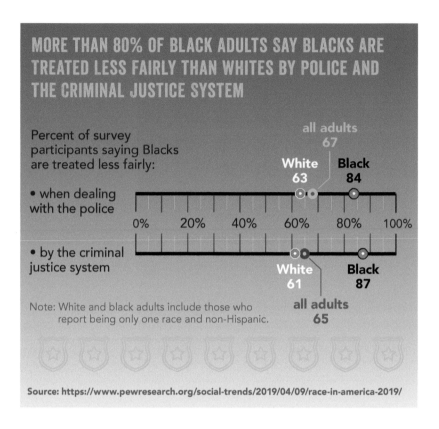

MORE THAN 80% OF BLACK ADULTS SAY BLACKS ARE TREATED LESS FAIRLY THAN WHITES BY POLICE AND THE CRIMINAL JUSTICE SYSTEM

Percent of survey participants saying Blacks are treated less fairly:

- when dealing with the police

all adults 67
White 63
Black 84

0%   20%   40%   60%   80%   100%

- by the criminal justice system

White 61
Black 87

all adults 65

Note: White and black adults include those who report being only one race and non-Hispanic.

Source: https://www.pewresearch.org/social-trends/2019/04/09/race-in-america-2019/

A mounting list of Black men and boys who have been killed by the police in high-profile incidents include Oscar Grant in Oakland; Freddie Gray in Baltimore, Maryland; Michael Brown in Ferguson, Missouri; Walter Scott in North Charleston, North Carolina; Tamir Rice in Cleveland, Ohio; Philando Castile in Falcon Heights, Minnesota; Stephon Clark in Sacramento, California; George Floyd in Minneapolis; Kokou Christopher Fiafonou in Austin, Minnesota; and Ali Osman in Phoenix, Arizona.

The Say Her Name (#SayHerName) movement—launched in 2014 by the African American Policy Forum and the Center for Intersectionality and Social Policy Studies—highlights the stories of Black women who have been killed by the police and suffered police violence. In 2017 Alteria Woods, a twenty-one-year-old pharmacy technician in Indian River County, Florida, was shot and killed during a SWAT team raid of her boyfriend's home while lying down in their bedroom. In 2020 Breonna Taylor, a twenty-six-year-old emergency medical technician in Louisville, Kentucky, was fatally shot by police during a no-knock warrant entry into her home.

Native American communities also continue to face challenges about policing. They are disproportionately impacted in everything from deadly force encounters with the police to longer terms of incarceration. Police also kill, punish, and brutalize Native Americans at alarming rates. According to the Centers for Disease Control and Prevention, "Native Americans are 3.1 times more likely than white Americans

A sculpture honoring Breonna Taylor was on display in New York City's Union Square in October 2021.

During the June 2020 protests sparked by the police killing of George Floyd, this truck displayed both a poster of Floyd as well as a Native Lives Matter sign. Both movements aim to heighten awareness of the inequality reflected in the American justice system.

to be killed by law enforcement." Native Americans are overrepresented in the prison population at a rate of 38 percent above the national average. The representation of Native Americans in local jails is four times higher than the national average. Drawing upon the Black Lives Matter movement, activists launched Native Lives Matter in 2014 to raise awareness and address police violence and brutality against Native Americans.

Investigations point to serious concerns regarding racism within law enforcement. A 2015 FBI report concluded that white supremacists and other domestic extremist groups had active connections to law enforcement agencies across the United States. In 2019 the US Center for Investigative

Reporting found that hundreds of active and retired police officers were members of extremist groups on Facebook. Many Americans are concerned that these police officers use their position of power as a way to harass and brutalize communities of color.

Public Trust and Community Engagement

Research shows communities of color tend to distrust police. A 2013 study showed that nearly one-third of US-born Latinos and more than 50 percent of foreign-born Latinos would rather contact a church or community leader about crime than contact the police. A 2020 poll conducted by the Public Broadcasting Service (PBS) revealed that almost half of the Black community has little or no confidence that law enforcement treats people with different skin colors equally. This distrust is a result of the history of policing and how law enforcement enacts modern policing methods in their neighborhoods. Black men are 2.5 times more likely to be killed by police than white males. And one-third of unarmed individuals killed by the police are Black Americans. It seems logical to distrust police amidst allegations of police brutality and violence, corruption, and even fatal shootings.

"From the arrival of the first slaves in Jamestown in 1619 to the lynchings of the nineteenth and twentieth centuries to the present day—black boys and men have been unlawfully killed by those who are sworn to uphold the law and by vigilantes who took the law into their own hands."

—Angela Davis, author of Policing the Black Man

For many, there are concerns that police are not held accountable for abuse of power, police brutality, and the use of excessive force. The entire police force is judged by the perceptions of procedural justice or one's experience of the justice system. The general public is looking for the values of fairness, consistency, transparency, and accountability to be upheld, which happens when the individuals impacted by policing feel they are heard, seen, engaged, and respected. This provides an opportunity for the community to impact the system by being a part of creating solutions. The community and police can then work together to foster mutual respect and cooperation, so public perception views police as working with the community to promote public safety.

Research shows when policing is seen as legitimate, the community is more likely to participate and collaborate in advancing public safety. One way police departments

PERCEPTIONS OF FAIRNESS AND JUSTICE IN POLICING

Data from the Washington, DC-based Pew Research Center has shown concerns about Black individuals being treated less fairly than white individuals in encounters with the police and the overall criminal justice system. According to a 2019 survey, 84 percent of Black adults described Black people as being treated less fairly by police when compared to white individuals; 63 percent of white respondents agreed that the Black community is treated less fairly during police encounters. And 87 percent of Black respondents and 61 percent of white respondents said the US criminal justice system treats Black people less fairly.

can create this type of community participation is through citizen oversight councils. These groups are an external accountability system. They foster community participation in ensuring police accountability. And they represent the community impacted by these issues.

The lack of trust in policing is part of a broader skepticism of the criminal justice system. Communities of color experience disparities at every junction of the legal system. According to the Sentencing Project, one of every three Black boys born in the early 2000s is expected to go to prison in his lifetime, and one of every six Latinos faces the same risk in comparison to one of every seventeen white boys. More than half of students arrested in school are Black or Latino boys. Research shows that people of color have higher bail, receive harsher sentences, and are more likely to be arrested for the same crime as their white counterparts.

A San Francisco police officer assists an elderly woman across the street in San Francisco, California, in 2020.

CHAPTER 3

POLICING AND VISIONS FOR PUBLIC SAFETY

Twenty-first-century policing goes beyond solving crimes to address a wide range of community issues and social challenges, such as homelessness, substance abuse, domestic abuse, and gun violence. Different policing models emerged as a result of these expansive demands, and several historical models shaped modern policing practices. They deal with how police officers are trained as well as their duties, responsibilities, and day-to-day work. Each model has particular characteristics. Yet they all rely on technology, community perspectives, and creative problem-solving to achieve one goal: reducing crime.

Models of Policing

Most modern police departments have adopted a combination of models to guide the behavior and actions of police officers. To follow the model of medieval knights, police officers' key focus is to fight crime according to laws. Similar to how knights were loyal to the king's orders, law enforcement would prioritize law and order. This creates an image of a warrior in battle, with police working to fight criminals and illegal behavior. However, this approach is punitive, which means it is focused on punishing or penalizing those who commit crimes rather than on rehabilitation.

In a guardian model, law enforcement focuses on collaboration and community engagement, building partnerships with the community to address crime. Police officers are seen as a part of the community and are vested in the well-being of the people they serve. They work with community members to address criminal behavior and promote safe communities.

Another model of policing is a restorative justice framework. In this model the community and police work together to repair the harm when a crime occurs to bring healing and reconciliation.

Order Maintenance Policing

The order maintenance policing model is based on a theory of crime known as the broken windows theory. In a 1969 study

THE GUARDIAN MODEL OF POLICING

The Washington State Criminal Justice Training Commission chose a guardian model of police training under its executive director, Sue Rahr. In 2012 she raised the question, "Why are we training officers like soldiers?" She ended boot camp–style training where officers were berated for not being able to succeed at drills that were meant to be insurmountable. She removed posters that reflected wars and replaced them with a US Constitution mural and other encouraging messages about policing as a noble profession worthy of honor. She focused on changing organizational strategies and training models.

The images of warriors and guardians shape police training models. In a warrior model, officers are trained to act as a soldier who takes orders and perceives policing as a part of a battle. Fighting crime is treated like fighting a hostile enemy. Police are then an occupying force in a specific territory. In comparison, the guardian model supports community engagement. It fosters procedural justice by demonstrating the values of fairness, equity, and accountability. The guardian's role is to protect the community and build trust within the community to address criminal behavior.

by psychologist Philip Zimbardo of Stanford University, he put two abandoned cars in two different locations. He left the first vehicle in a "high crime," low-income neighborhood in New York City. After just ten minutes, people began vandalizing the car. They took car parts and destroyed the car. The second vehicle was placed in a wealthy neighborhood in Palo Alto, California. No one touched this second car for over a week. A week later, Zimbardo returned, smashed the car with a sledgehammer, and moved the car. Subsequently, passersby started to destroy the car, just as in New York City.

Philip Zimbardo, George Kelling, and James Wilson (*left to right*) all contributed to the creation of the theory of order maintenance.

This established the theory that a neighborhood with visible signs of disorder—crime or neglect or property damage—serves as an open invitation for more serious criminal behavior.

In 1982 criminologists George L. Kelling (Rutgers University) and James Q. Wilson (Harvard, UCLA) built upon Zimbardo's study. They wanted to use his theory to improve policing practices. They hypothesized that quickly addressing small signs of disorder in a community, such as broken windows, loitering, and graffiti, would discourage petty crime and prevent escalation to serious crimes. According to the theory of order maintenance, police should mainly focus resources on maintaining order in communities instead of on solving major, severe crimes.

The order maintenance policing model has its critics. Many social scientists argue that this model does not address the real root cause of crime—poverty. "The broken-windows theory magically reverses the well-understood causal relationship between crime and poverty, arguing that poverty and social disorganization are the result, not the cause, of crime," writes Brooklyn College sociologist Alex S. Vitale in his 2021 book *The End of Policing*.

Some people, including Kelling and Wilson, argue that the order maintenance model can enable discriminatory behavior. In their initial 1982 article, Kelling and Wilson wrote, "How do we ensure . . . that the police do not become the agents of neighborhood bigotry? We can offer no wholly satisfactory answer to this important question." In practice, communities of color have been disproportionately impacted by the order maintenance policing model.

In 1993 the mayor of New York City, Rudy Giuliani, adopted order maintenance policing to address high crime rates. An additional 3,660 police officers were hired to patrol communities and address homelessness and minor crimes. New York City saw a sharp increase in stop and frisk, stopping someone for questioning and patting them down, which was later deemed unconstitutional.

According to a 2021 report, there were 8,947 stops in the year. The stops included 5,404 Black people (60 percent) and 2,457 Latinx (27 percent). More than half of those stopped were found to be innocent (61 percent). Even beyond stop and frisk, people of color face significantly more summonses for minor offenses, such as disorderly conduct, loitering, and failure to have a dog licensed, than white people. Some argue that racial bias led to more harmful police encounters and did not address the underlying crime issues in local communities.

Hot Spot Policing

Hot spot policing emerged in the 1980s and 1990s as a targeted approach that uses technology. In this model,

Stop-and-frisk policies involve a two-step process. First, a police officer stops and interrogates a pedestrian. Then, if the officer believes the pedestrian may possess illegal materials, the officer searches the person for drugs or weapons.

police use computerized police mapping, drones, algorithms, analysis software, and advanced cameras to identify key problem areas, collect data, evaluate challenges, and develop a strategic plan of action. Police use data such as 911 emergency calls to understand when and how crime emerges in real time and to predict when and where crimes may occur. Police officers are then assigned to specific areas where data identifies high crime rates. Officers patrol these areas during high-risk times—whether it be the early morning, midday, or late evening. Nine out of ten US police departments are using crime mapping to identify and address areas with high levels of crime.

Modern police practices also use intelligence-led policing. According to the US Department of Justice, intelligence-led policing is "a collaborative law enforcement approach combining problem-solving policing, information sharing, and police accountability, with enhanced intelligence operations." This type of policing focuses on identifying repeat offenders and potential victims. Police then focus on developing strategies for preventing future victimization before it occurs.

In 2011 Mayor Greg Davis of Southaven, Mississippi, demonstrated a crime-mapping tool used to show where crimes had occurred. Police use data like this to identify areas they may direct crime prevention efforts.

This approach focuses on strategic problem-solving and coordination between other law enforcement agencies. For instance, a local police department may work with the FBI, the Department of Homeland Security, and a community to address a crime trend. This provides access to additional information and data.

Problem-Oriented Policing

In 1979 University of Wisconsin–Madison criminologist Herman Goldstein introduced problem-oriented policing (POP). This model seeks to prevent crime by addressing root causes in the community. Goldstein challenged law enforcement to reevaluate the tools in their toolbox. He pointed out that effective crime-fighting involves more than arrests. Instead of identifying patterns in crime and analyzing data, POP focuses on understanding the issues within a community that might motivate people to commit crimes. For example, an increase in drug trafficking may be connected to a lack of economic opportunities or social services in a particular community. Once police understand the underlying issues facing the community, they can implement strategies to address them.

Goldstein recognized that policing is a part of the broader social fabric of the community. The police alone cannot address the complexities of the challenges affecting the community.

Community Policing

Community policing focuses on building collaborative relationships between police officers and other community members. The vast majority of police departments use community policing in their organizational strategy.

Herman Goldstein was a professor of law at the University of Wisconsin–Madison. He is pictured here at the university in 1976.

CRIME STOPPERS

Crime Stoppers is a crime-fighting partnership with police, media, and community members. People provide tips about crimes and are eligible for rewards. Founded in 1976 by a detective in Albuquerque, New Mexico, it has expanded around the world with over twenty thousand chapters. Crime Stoppers has led to 812,105 arrests and seizures of drugs and stolen property estimated at $1,260,430,307.

Traditionally, a police officer would be assigned to patrol a specific geographic area known as a beat. Beat cops monitor traffic and respond to reported crime in a neighborhood. This model allows the community to participate in shaping the goals of their local police department, problem-solving and building long-term relationships with law enforcement. Officers spend significant amounts of time establishing and maintaining relationships with community members to prevent crime. An officer might greet residents and business owners, inquire about their days, and explore ways to foster community building. The officer would learn not only about the criminal justice challenges within a community but also its strengths—maybe the neighborhood is home to a thriving refugee community or has an arts magnet middle school. These assets can be used to build more connected and stronger communities. The officer would then work with the community to strengthen the social fabric of the neighborhood.

In a community policing model, the success of policing is not measured by the number of arrests officers make. Instead, the goal is to reduce crime and increase community connections. An officer is considered successful if they are engaged and have created lasting relationships with the community they serve.

Community engagement can help police become fully invested in the future of public safety. One such approach is focusing on values-based policing. Values are guiding principles that bring people together to create a shared vision for the future. This type of model places core values at the center of police and community interactions and engagement. It honors the sanctity of life, establishes accountability, promotes trust, and ensures legitimacy. It is anchored in unity and human dignity. These values would guide police training and practices from communication with community members to policies that protect lives. Values-based policing provides key guiding principles that support community building and engagement.

"Community policing is a philosophy that promotes organizational strategies that support the systematic use of partnerships and problem-solving techniques to proactively address the immediate conditions that give rise to public safety issues such as crime, social disorder, and fear of crime."

—Office of Community Oriented Policing Services, US Department of Justice

The national hub for community policing was established in 1994 with the launch of the Community Oriented Policing Services. The office is part of the US Department of Justice and was formed through the Violent Crime Control and Law Enforcement Act of 1994. The office advances a national vision of public safety, supports school crime prevention efforts, and develops solutions to crime.

This model combines organizational transformation and building community partnerships to lead to change in the community. The combination supports safe communities and fosters strong families. Since its inception, the office has granted over $14 billion to support community policing efforts within local police departments. Funds are distributed directly to police departments to meet their community needs. This may include hiring additional officers, helping to reduce gun violence, and offering crisis support to those in need.

Taking It to the Big Screen: Hollywood and Policing

The issue of police violence in the United States took center stage with the release of the film *Fruitvale Station*. The 2013 film documented the final hours of Oscar Grant's life in Oakland, on New Year's Day 2009. A Black screenwriter and director, Ryan Coogler, wanted to make a difference by focusing his film career on social justice issues. He used his film debut to highlight the injustices experienced by the Black community during violent police encounters. The film begins with twenty-two-year-old Grant going through his normal daily routine and ending the day with friends as they celebrate the beginning of the new year.

That night Grant and his friends were taking the Bay Area Rapid Transit train when police were called for an alleged fight on a crowded train returning from San Francisco. Security officers removed Grant and his friends from the train. Police then detained them. Transit officer Johannes Mehserle shot and killed Grant while he was lying on his stomach. Witnesses recorded the incident at the train station. Mehserle later claimed that he was reaching for a Taser and not a gun. The jury found him guilty of involuntary manslaughter, and he was sentenced to a two-year prison term and spent eleven months in prison.

This video recording was one of the first of a police killing to go viral and draw national attention. It was uploaded to the web and released on other media outlets. Grant's murder led to months of protests in Oakland and beyond. Protesters chanted in the street, "We are Oscar Grant." This message raised awareness of the historical pain and trauma in communities of color. It was not about only one individual. It was about the threat of police violence so many feel.

Director Ryan Coogler attends TheWrap's 2013 Awards and Foreign Screening Series during a screening of his movie *Fruitvale Station* in Los Angeles.

The film won many awards and accolades while also drawing national attention to police violence and its impact on Black Americans. Grant's mother, Wanda Johnson, has continued to advocate for change in policing policies. She supports at-risk youth in creating new pathways to support their well-being. She works with other families to fight for justice for loved ones who have been killed by the police. She also leads the Oscar Grant Foundation, which seeks to bridge the gap between young Black men and law enforcement.

Protesters in New York City hold hands during a prayer in the days following the death of Eric Garner in July 2014.

CHAPTER 4

REIMAGINING AND TRANSFORMING POLICING

Eric Garner's death caused by New York City police in July 2014 ignited protests across the nation. A cell phone video recorded by his friend Ramsey Orta of the deadly police encounter was watched millions of times on social media. It captured an escalating exchange between two officers and Garner in Staten Island, New York. One of the officers then placed Garner in a choke hold. A choke hold is used to restrain someone by restricting or cutting off either a person's breathing or the flow of oxygen to the brain. This type of restraint can be lethal and is illegal in New York. In the video, Garner can be heard repeatedly saying "I can't breathe." He eventually lost consciousness and soon after died at a hospital.

Eric Garner was a forty-six-year-old father of six who was known as a "neighborhood peacemaker" in his community. Police stopped him for allegedly selling single cigarettes on the street without collecting sales tax, which is illegal in New York. This was not Garner's first encounter with the police. He was stopped, searched, and harassed by the police on a regular basis. In 2007, for example, Garner filed a lawsuit claiming that police had routinely violated his civil rights. He said he had been humiliated and sexually assaulted by police in public. That July day in 2014, he said to the police who stopped him, "Every time you see me you arrest me. I'm tired of it. It stops today."

After Garner's death, protesters organized across the nation. During the protests, people marched in solidarity to address police violence. They chanted in unison "I can't breathe" to honor Garner. They were determined to hold police departments accountable and to ban choke holds across the nation.

The protesters wanted to see immediate policy changes in police departments. These changes would protect lives by eliminating excessive force. Excessive force is when force is used beyond what is needed to control a situation. Protesters took to social media and used the hashtag #BlackLivesMatter to seek justice for the Garner family and demand police reform to end deadly force. BLM helped to organize the community for change. Young people, community elders, teachers, and parents came together to advocate for policy change and to build a shared vision of public safety.

Why Do People Protest?

Protesting is standing up for what you believe in. People lift their voices for justice by peacefully marching, singing songs or chanting, and holding up their fists together in solidarity. Protesting is a method of nonviolent resistance, like boycotting, sit-ins, and petitions.

Protest is also a strategy for challenging a system and creating change. During the Silent Protest Parade of 1917, nearly ten thousand African Americans marched in Harlem, a neighborhood in New York City. Children and women dressed in white to symbolize the innocence of the Black community

In July 1917, an estimated ten thousand protesters marched through the streets of New York City in what is know an the Silent Protest Parade.

killed in East Saint Louis, Illinois, that year. They were killed for filling vacant jobs left by white workers during labor strikes. That year Black people were lynched in Memphis, Tennessee, and Waco, Texas. Marchers silently held signs that read, "Make America Safe for Democracy" and "Thou shalt not kill." This was one of the first mass protests in US history. From the civil rights movement to today, protesting has been key to mobilizing for change.

Black Lives Matter

"Black Lives Matter" has become the unifying message of protesters who have grown tired of seeing the senseless killings of Black people by the police and vigilantes. In 2012 seventeen-year-old Trayvon Martin was walking home from a store in Sanford, Florida. He encountered the neighborhood watch captain, George Zimmerman, who called 911 and reported Martin as a suspicious person. Zimmerman confronted Martin and then shot and killed him. The Martin family launched a petition on Change.org calling for Zimmerman's arrest. He was charged with second-degree murder but was acquitted.

In 2013 Alicia Garza first used the phrase "Black Lives Matter" in a Facebook post. She was tired of seeing Black people killed and felt there was no justice. She was outraged that Martin's killer was not found guilty. Her friend,

"We have a right to protest for what is right. That's all we can do. There are people hurting, there are people suffering, so we have an obligation, a mandate, to do something."

—Representative John Lewis, 2016

Patrisse Cullors, added a hashtag, #BlackLivesMatter, which went viral on social media. Garza, Cullors, and Ayo Tometi founded Black Lives Matter Global Network to voice the many injustices in the Black community. This was the birth of a global movement for justice for the Black community, demanding the honor, respect, and protection of the rights of Black people.

> "black people. I love you. I love us. Our lives matter."
>
> —Alicia Garza, BLM cofounder

Millions around the world have joined this coalition for "freedom, liberation and justice." They share common goals of protecting the humanity of all Black people and ensuring Black lives are not systematically targeted but instead honored and protected.

Black Lives Matter was posted on social media an average of 3.7 million times per day following George Floyd's death in 2020. The hashtag was shared on Twitter more than 50 million times between January 28, 2013, and April 30, 2021. Additionally, a call to defund the police appeared on social media and in the streets.

Reform the Police

Racial bias, police brutality, and lax disciplinary action for officers with a history of violent encounters have led civilians to call for increased police accountability. Some protesters, activists, and government officials seek to reform police departments. Their goal is to ensure the safety and well-being of community members while also protecting their rights. Some reform advocates argue that policy changes and additional training can help improve community and police relations. While others envision hiring such professionals as a commissioner of public safety to guide reform and address the needs of a community to prevent crime.

USE OF FORCE

Many police reforms focus on limiting when police can use force and what level of force they can use. Enacting restrictive use of force policies has been shown to reduce instances of police violence.

Most law enforcement agencies have policies that guide their use of force. These guidelines are known as the use of force continuum, and they outline responses an officer should take based on the level of danger they perceive in a particular situation. This continuum ranges from an officer being present to the use of lethal force. The use of force continuum serves as a guide to determine what level of force should be used in a given situation. Some situations can be addressed with a verbal warning, while others may require additional action from an officer. For example, an officer may use force to stop a violent crime or use a verbal warning to address an argument between neighbors.

The US Supreme Court set the standard for reasonable use of force in the 1989 case *Graham v. Connor*. The court ruled that the use of force must be considered reasonable if another reasonable officer would use the same level of force in the same situation. Some believe that this ruling gives officers too much power, since the definition of "reasonable" to an officer and "reasonable" to a community member may be different.

De-escalation tactics are a tool often promoted by reform advocates. De-escalation tactics in policing refer to strategies and techniques employed by law enforcement officers to minimize and defuse potentially volatile situations, with the goal of reducing the need for force or violence.

TASK FORCE ON 21ST CENTURY POLICING

In 2014 President Obama commissioned the Task Force on 21st Century Policing to address challenges in policing while restoring community trust. Local government, law enforcement, and community members met to create change. The task force's final recommendations were published in a report on six key areas: building trust and legitimacy, policy and oversight, technology and social media, community policing and crime reduction, training and education, and officer wellness and safety.

The task force created fifty-nine recommendations and outlined ninety-two strategies. Strategies include hosting community gatherings to listen and learn from one another, conducting surveys on community perspectives on policing, defining and building the structure for a civilian overview council, and addressing the needs of the community by focusing on ending poverty and unemployment.

President Barack Obama (*center*) sits with cochairs of the newly created Task Force on 21st Century Policing in Washington, DC, in November 2014.

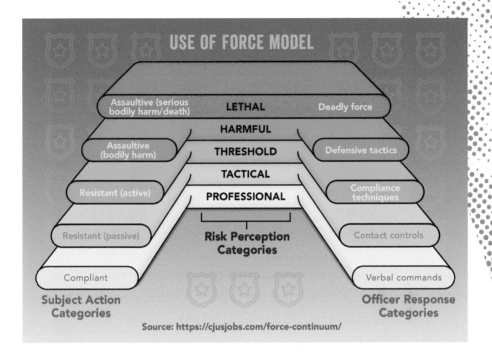

USE OF FORCE MODEL

Subject Action Categories	Risk Perception Categories	Officer Response Categories
Assaultive (serious bodily harm/death)	LETHAL	Deadly force
	HARMFUL	
Assaultive (bodily harm)	THRESHOLD	Defensive tactics
	TACTICAL	
Resistant (active)	PROFESSIONAL	Compliance techniques
Resistant (passive)		Contact controls
Compliant		Verbal commands

Source: https://cjusjobs.com/force-continuum/

The primary objective of de-escalation is to ensure the safety of all individuals involved, including the officers, suspects, and bystanders.

De-escalation tactics typically involve effective communication, active listening, and the use of nonthreatening body language. Officers may employ techniques such as calmly speaking to individuals, maintaining a respectful and empathetic demeanor, providing clear and concise instructions, and attempting to establish rapport and trust. They may also utilize time and distance to allow for a cooler heads prevail approach, providing opportunities for individuals to calm down and reassess the situation.

The aim of de-escalation is to create a more peaceful and cooperative atmosphere, reducing the likelihood of conflicts escalating into violence. It emphasizes the use of verbal persuasion and conflict resolution skills over physical force. De-escalation tactics are part of a broader approach to community-oriented policing, fostering positive relationships and mutual understanding between law enforcement and the communities they serve. Research in Louisville, Kentucky, found when officers receive de-escalation training, it reduced use-of-force situations by 28 percent and citizens being injured by 26 percent. Officer injuries were reduced by 36 percent.

Laws banning choke holds have passed in many states. These changes in the law are to protect the community from police violence. For instance, the sponsor of the bill in Utah banning knee-on-neck choke holds, Representative Sandra Hollins, explained that the community was feeling unsafe. She introduced the bill to acknowledge the concerns of the community and bring meaningful change. Notably, Hollins is the only Black member of the Utah legislature.

Some police departments have adopted duty to intervene policies. These policies require officers to act when they witness another officer using unnecessary or excessive force or engaging in misconduct. Duty to intervene policies aim to promote accountability, prevent abuses of power, and ensure the safety and well-being of individuals involved in police encounters. Community groups also often call for an end to qualified immunity, which protects a police officer from being legally liable for their actions taken in the course of their official duties, unless those actions violate constitutional rights. The officer's city or jurisdiction can be sued for behavior that can cause injury or death but not the individual officer. Many characterize this as a police officer having zero accountability for their actions, arguing that it allows police officers to avoid accountability for wrongdoing and undermines efforts to hold law enforcement accountable for excessive force and other misconduct.

Following the murder of George Floyd, the Minnesota legislature passed the Minnesota Police Accountability Act of 2020. This law modified the threshold for the police use of deadly force and required

> all law enforcement agencies to update their written policies on the use of force to include the requirements of 1) Duty to Intervene in excessive force situations; 2) Duty to Report illegal use of force; and 3) an officer must first consider less lethal measures before applying deadly force.

Additionally, all law enforcement agencies must report to the Minnesota Bureau of Criminal Apprehension (BCA) all incidents of use of force that result in serious bodily injury or death, and the Ensuring Police Excellence and Improving Community Relations Advisory Council was established to promote community engagement.

Several states have created task forces, commissions, and other working groups to build a new vision for policing reform and improve community relations. One such example is Minnesota's Working Group on Police-Involved Deadly Force Encounters. In 2019 cochairs Minnesota attorney general Keith Ellison and Public Safety commissioner John Harrington launched this state initiative to bring together a group of professionals from the community, education, judicial branch, and law enforcement who were seeking to reduce deadly force encounters through a holistic approach. The overall goal was to change policing practices and procedures.

The working group developed a blueprint for action. Four hearings and three listening sessions between August

2019 and January 2020 were held across Minnesota. Family members shared their stories of loss, pain, and trauma, experts outlined best practices for reform, and police officers shared the reality of policing. The group's final work was a report that outlined twenty-eight recommendations and thirty-eight action steps. This included the following:

- Establish a formal, protected, non-disciplinary Sentinel Event Review process . . . to review critical incidents and identify systemic issues that need to be addressed to improve outcomes.
- [D]iscuss strategies to increase the role of the POST [Peace Officer Standards and Training] Board to approve, suspend, or revoke officer licenses at the Chief Law Enforcement Officer's request.

TRAINING

Police reform activists regularly advocate for expanding and improving officer training. In the early 1900s, Chief August Vollmer emphasized the importance of higher education and additional training for police officers. Most jurisdictions require at least a high school diploma, while others seek police candidates with at least some college education or a four-year college degree.

Higher education has been seen as a tool to support learning and growth from problem-solving to communication skills, and aspiring police officers receive additional training after completing their degrees in college through the police academy. On average in the United States there is a twenty-one-week program (over five hundred hours) before an officer is out on patrol, which is significantly less than in other

Baltimore, Maryland, police officer Edward Gillespie lectures to in-service officers during a Fairness and Impartiality in Policing Implicit Bias training class in November 2015.

developed countries. In Finland, police training is fifty-five hundred hours, and in Germany over four thousand hours.

Current training models emphasize firearm skills and self-defense. While the ability to defend oneself is an important skill, critics believe that officer training should have a more holistic, community-centered approach that includes significant amounts of conflict management training. This type of training recognizes the role of the police to protect and serve while ensuring the least amount of force is used to fulfill these duties. It includes learning de-escalation techniques and strengthening problem-solving skills.

Implicit bias education is another reform effort. Implicit biases are automatic associations people make between groups of people and stereotypes about those groups. A person may not be aware they have these biases, and they may contradict a person's consciously held values. Implicit bias can impact how police interact with community members. They may unconsciously focus suspicion on some while presuming innocence in others. Implicit bias training provides guidance on how to challenge one's own and others' implicit biases. The goal is to improve procedural justice (perception of fairness in interactions with law enforcement) and foster trust between police and the community.

Some training models include leadership development to empower police officers to make changes within their departments and society. These programs typically aim to cultivate leadership traits such as decision-making, problem-solving, communication, adaptability, ethical conduct, community engagement, cultural competency, and the ability to inspire and motivate others. The purpose of police training leadership development is to equip law enforcement professionals with the skills and competencies needed to lead their teams, make sound judgments, and effectively respond to the dynamic challenges they encounter in their roles. By investing in leadership development, police departments seek to foster a positive and accountable organizational culture, enhance officer performance, and improve community relations.

NO-KNOCK WARRANTS

A no-knock warrant occurs when police obtain a search warrant to enter a home or other building without first knocking or making their presence known. Police use this type of warrant when there is fear that evidence related to an investigation may be destroyed if they do not take swift action, when police officers have reason to believe that they need to fear for their safety, or when a suspect could escape.

No-knock warrants pose significant risks to both law enforcement officers and the occupants of the premises. The element of surprise can lead to confusion, heightened tension, and potential violence. Due to the quick and unannounced nature of no-knock warrants, there is a higher likelihood of mistaken identity or errors in the execution of the warrant. They also raise concerns about the violation of Fourth Amendment rights protecting against unreasonable searches and seizures. The element of surprise and the absence of notification undermine individuals' ability to exercise their constitutional rights and potentially lead to excessive use of force. The sudden intrusion into a person's

Protesters demonstrate outside the Hennepin County Government Center in April 2022 in Minneapolis. Police shot Amir Locke after entering his cousin's apartment with a no-knock warrant.

home can create a high-stress situation, and residents may react defensively or fear for their safety, leading to confrontations that could result in injury or loss of life.

Breonna's Law was passed in Kentucky after public outcry following the death of Breonna Taylor. The law signed by the governor prohibited the use of no-knock warrants except in limited circumstances. Minneapolis mayor Jacob Frey placed a moratorium, or suspension, on no-knock warrants after the police shot and killed twenty-two-year-old Amir Locke. Between 2010 and 2016, ninety-four people (eighty-one civilians and thirteen officers) were killed in the US during no-knock warrant police raids. Some reform efforts included officers wearing uniforms to be clearly identifiable, waiting to enter a premise (with wait times of fifteen to thirty seconds after announcing police are on the scene), and additional verification of the specific residence to identify who lives in the home.

Advocates argue that such alternative approaches can help mitigate the dangers associated with no-knock warrants while still allowing law enforcement to effectively carry out their duties. Law enforcement raises concerns about process and safety risks under a ban. Judges issue search warrants so there are multiple layers of oversight before a no-knock warrant can be issued.

DATA COLLECTION

Police departments are developing tools to improve data collection with the goal of keeping the community informed and engaged. Data provides a visual tool for monitoring and evaluating policing from claims of excessive force to the rate of traffic stops. By making data more readily accessible, police leaders hope to promote transparency and accountability while building public trust.

BODY CAMERAS

Body cameras are small recording devices worn by police officers. They document the interactions between an officer and an individual by providing audio and visual evidence, which increases transparency and accountability. It also can deter officers and civilians from illegal behavior by promoting de-escalation. Body camera footage can serve as valuable evidence in criminal investigations, and it can also be used as a training tool to evaluate officer performance and identify areas for improvement. Interpretation of body camera footage can be subjective, and biases may influence how the footage is perceived or used as evidence. But police officers do not always have their cameras on, and officers have control over when to activate or deactivate body cameras. This limits whether all interactions are recorded and later available for review. Seven states mandate wearing a body camera, while thirty-four other states and the District of Columbia are working on mandate legislation.

This Seattle police detective wears an Axon body camera on their uniform.

Some believe wearing body cameras helps to protect community members from violence and abuse of power. Others believe it ensures officers can avoid false allegations since the entire interaction is being captured in real time. Yet research shows conflicting accounts about the effectiveness of wearing body cameras. Some reports demonstrate that a body camera may have little to no impact in reducing claims of excessive force. A 2021 study showed when using body cameras, excessive force can be reduced by at least 10 percent. Some argue that the presence of body cameras can change officer behavior where officers become overly cautious or hesitant, potentially impacting their effectiveness in high-stress situations. Finally, body cameras require significant financial resources for equipment, data storage, maintenance, and policy development.

CRISIS INTERVENTION TEAMS

According to the National Alliance on Mental Illness (NAMI), one in five Americans live with mental illness and one in twenty are experiencing severe mental illness. Police are often dispatched to address emergency calls related to mental illness, but police officers typically lack the specialized training to deal with individuals experiencing mental health crises, which can lead to confrontations. Nearly a quarter of people killed by police since 2015 have a known mental illness. Even when incidents do not end in violence, people in these cases may be treated in ways that result in harmful rather than helpful outcomes. One alternative may be a separate crisis hotline rather than 911 alone. This would offer individualized support and address an episode without criminalizing it. According to Angela Kimball of the National Alliance on Mental Illness, this alternative would be effective since there's

Somerville, Massachusetts, police chief Dave Fallon spoke to law enforcement officers after a training at the Somerville-Cambridge-NAMI Regional Crisis Intervention Team Training and Technical Assistance Center in 2016.

a mobile crisis team of behavioral health professionals who can help defuse the situation, connect people to treatment and get them on a path to recovery."

National attention on this issue arose in the response to the death of Daniel Prude, a forty-one-year-old Black man in Rochester, New York. In March 2020, his brother called for the support of law enforcement when Prude was having a mental breakdown, and his brother was concerned that he would accidentally harm himself. When police arrived, Prude was handcuffed, and a hood was placed over his head. Three officers pinned him to the ground and pressed his head against the street for two minutes. He stopped breathing and had to be resuscitated. He was hospitalized and a week later was taken off life support and died.

Reform advocates have requested investment from police departments and cities in crisis intervention teams who are trained to reduce harm during mental health crises. Some police departments have created teams that consist of social workers, psychologists, and other crisis managers that aid in responding to calls when there are mental health needs. These teams train police officers on how best to respond to calls involving mental illness. Other cities create special task forces to conduct research and provide recommendations for how police can better address mental health crises. In 2011 a task force in San Francisco developed new training that provided officers with approaches to de-escalate mental health crises. These types of task forces include mental health service providers and users, advocates, criminal justice system employees, and community members.

RESIDENCY REQUIREMENTS

To support community policing models, some advocates want to establish residency requirements for police officers, which would require police officers to live in the communities where they work. The theory is that officers will be more engaged with the community if they live there and that they will be more familiar with the issues that face that community. On average, 40 percent of police officers live in the communities that they serve. But this number can vary widely. In Minneapolis only 8 percent of the city's police officers live within the city limits. Some police forces already have a residency requirement. Others offer incentives for moving into the community such as extra points on the entrance exam for new recruits.

FEDERAL POLICY CHANGES

The George Floyd Justice in Policing Act was first introduced in Congress in 2020. The federal legislation outlined a framework for nationwide policing reform. Several common reforms are included in the bill, including a ban on no-knock warrants for federal drug investigations, prohibition of choke holds, and required use of body cameras. The bill would also restrict qualified immunity, making it easier to find officers personally liable for violating a civilian's civil rights, and establish a national registry compiling officer misconduct complaints, disciplinary records, and termination records. While the act passed in the Democrat-controlled House of Representatives in 2021, negotiations in the Senate stalled because Republicans and Democrats could not agree on qualified immunity and the national database.

> **"I'm tired. I'm tired of the pain I'm feeling now and I'm tired of the pain I feel every time another black person is killed for no reason. . . . I'm here today to ask you to make it stop. Stop the pain. Stop us from being tired."**
>
> *—Philonise Floyd, George Floyd's brother*

Police reform requires leadership, commitment to change, and money. For example, in Minnesota the state government and private sector came together to make some reform efforts possible. To do so, the proposed Minnesota 2021–2023 budget included $4.2 million for implementing working group recommendations for supporting community healing and officer wellness (Minnesota HEALS [Hope, Education, and Law and Safety] program, and fostering innovation in policing. The Pohlad Family Foundation committed $3 million in partnership with the National League of Cities for these recommendations. Yet some believe additional funding should not be invested in policing and could be put to better use by investing in community programming.

Defunding the Police

One of the most controversial suggestions for police reform is known as defunding the police. This type of reform would take money from a police budget and move it to other areas of need—such as job development, mental health services, and affordable housing in a community. In 2019, $123 billion were spent on policing in the United States. In many cities, one of the largest items of a city's budget is policing. For example, Houston, Texas, allocated $954 million to its police department in fiscal year 2021, about 19 percent of the total budget. In Raleigh, North Carolina, 21 percent of funds are spent on policing, and in Billings, Montana, 64 percent. Nationally, the US spends twice as much on the criminal justice system (police, prisons, and courts) than on cash

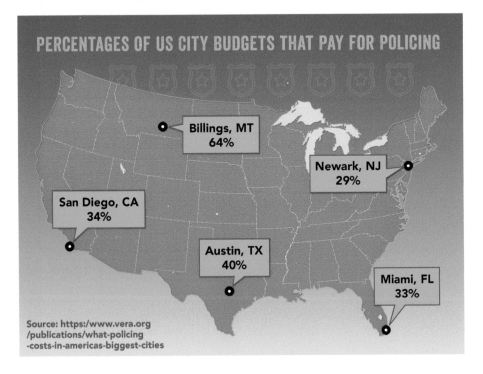

PERCENTAGES OF US CITY BUDGETS THAT PAY FOR POLICING

Billings, MT
64%

Newark, NJ
29%

San Diego, CA
34%

Austin, TX
40%

Miami, FL
33%

Source: https:/www.vera.org
/publications/what-policing
-costs-in-americas-biggest-cities

Minneapolis City Council member Alondra Cano spoke to community members at the Path Forward meeting at Powderhorn Park in Minneapolis in June 2020. Many city leaders and concerned citizens are looking for ways to change the face of policing.

welfare benefits (food stamps, supplemental social security, and Temporary Assistance for Needy Families).

Reallocating police funding is not a new idea. In 1967 President Johnson's Commission on Law Enforcement and Administration of Justice recommended changing funding priorities to invest in low-income, underserved, and marginalized communities. The report's summary stated that "crime cannot be controlled without the interest and participation of schools, businesses, social agencies, private groups, and individual citizens." The report also said that addressing social and economic pressures, such as creating affordable housing, funding neighborhood schools, and providing access to health services, can reduce crime in a community. Many criminologists and community advocates agree that investing in practical strategies to meet the

Artist Neal Skorpen depicts strategies for addressing community challenges in this comic.

basic needs of community members is the best crime prevention strategy.

Defunding efforts also seek to address mental health crises. Families have advocated for additional resources to protect their loved ones when they experience mental illness crises. One way to acquire these resources would be for a city to reallocate police funding to hire professionals with specialized training to address mental health crises. A crisis management team could work within a police force, or it could be an independent mental health program in the community. Either one allows police officers an opportunity to focus on violent crime and avoid addressing crisis management, which they are not trained to address. Mental health advocates such as psychiatrist Saadia Sediqzadah

ADDRESSING GUN VIOLENCE IN CHICAGO

Chicago, Illinois, has a high rate of gun violence. During the summer of 2021, more than sixteen hundred people were victims of gun violence during a domestic dispute, conflict, or fight. Some believe additional policing services will reduce this violence. The budget of the Chicago Police Department in 2021 was $1.7 billion. This is more than the city's budget for community services and infrastructure combined. Others believe the policing budget should be reduced and the funds should be reinvested in community services.

Police shootings are also a part of this cycle of violence. Laquan McDonald, Rekia Boyd, RonnieMan Johnson, and many others were killed in officer-involved shootings in the city. Chicago alderperson Jeanette Taylor is an advocate for defunding the police. As a Black woman, she draws on her personal experience in describing policing. She encourages "defunding a system that hates us and kills us on a consistent basis." Taylor has a vision of a vibrant community built on livable wage jobs, affordable health care, and quality education. This would require an investment of city resources in resources needed in the community. Taylor makes the case that the city is not broke but that community needs are not being prioritized and that resources are poorly managed. According to several Chicago alderpersons, including Taylor, "It's time for our city to seriously look at cutting the police budget and directing those funds to the public programs that will support working-class and poor Chicagoans."

support the reallocation of resources. She says that in a medical emergency, an ambulance shows up, and having police respond to mental health crises is like "criminalizing mental illness." The Crisis Assistance Helping Out on the

Streets program in Eugene, Oregon, addresses these challenges. The program sends unarmed responders to address mental health and drug-related issues instead of dispatching the police. Of 24,000 calls in 2019, only 150 required police backup. This means the responders were able to meet the needs of people in crisis with drastically reduced reliance on policing. The defunding strategy is shifting funding from policing to direct community services for specific types of calls.

The common misconception about defunding police is that it is anti-police. But the focus of this type of reform is to explore how to allocate resources across different types of community services in a way that benefits the people being served.

Disband the Police

The call to disband the police focuses on the elimination of a police department or a particular unit of law enforcement. Another organization would be created to address and uphold public safety through a community-based approach. Some community members support disbanding to create a way for community voices to be heard. They believe that current police services are no longer necessary or that they are not an effective approach to public safety. Others say that policing is a key tool for ensuring safety, so the organization and structure should be kept.

In the early 2010s, Camden, New Jersey, was experiencing great challenges with their police force and violent crime. The city had the highest crime rate in the United States in 2012, with a murder rate eighteen times higher than the national average. Camden's police department was disbanded in 2013 and replaced with the Camden County Police Department.

Black officers in Camden, New Jersey, join community activists for a rally hosted by Black Men Rising in June 13, 2020.

About 40 percent of officers who worked for the city department were hired into the new county department, including the police chief. Police Chief J. Scott Thomson asked his officers to focus on serving the community. "We were going to have all of our officers have the identity of guardians and not warriors," he said in an interview. They held cookouts, made personal connections, and sponsored events with the community. Camden's policing model went viral in 2015 after an arrest of a man wielding a knife. The officers surrounded him until they could take him into custody instead of following the typical protocol—taking a suspect into custody through force—that might have ended in the man being shot and killed by the police. Camden has successfully decreased the rates of violent crimes and has since become a model for other cities seeking policing reform in partnership with the community.

In June of 2020, the Minneapolis City Council voted to amend the city charter to allow for a proposal to disband the Minneapolis Police Department following the murder of George Floyd. The proposal sought to replace the department with "a department of community safety and violence prevention" that used "a holistic, public-health-oriented approach." The new department allowed for a law enforcement division with police officers but also included support for mental health, domestic abuse, and additional social services. After the proposal, the issue was left for the voters to decide.

The issue was put before voters in November 2021, but 56 percent of Minneapolis voters opposed the proposal to disband the police. Some voters thought there was a lack of a specific plan. Others were concerned about addressing ongoing issues about crime in the streets. Crime rates in Minneapolis went up in the year and a half between when the city council expressed their commitment to disband the force and when the question went on the ballot. Some worried that crime would worsen with fewer officers and resources and that the number of officers needed to be maintained or even increased. But city officials and employees had been exploring what was the future of public safety and how to move forward. After the proposal failed, the city continued to work toward changes in public safety. They prioritized three areas: alternatives to police response, violence prevention, and police policy reform. These efforts include the development of a 911-based mental health first responder program and behavioral response team support that can address challenges in the communities.

REFORMING THE MPD

Following the murder of George Floyd in 2020, the Minnesota Department of Human Rights (MDHR) filed a discrimination charge against the City of Minneapolis and the Minneapolis Police Department (MPD). The MDHR investigated whether the city was practicing a pattern of racial discrimination in policing, which would be a violation of the Minnesota Human Rights Act.

After a two-year investigation, the MDHR reported that the city had practiced pattern discrimination. They worked with city officials to create a settlement agreement reforming the city's policing framework. The agreement outlines ways to decrease aggressive tactics such as use of force, reduce discrimination and police misconduct, support wellness among officers, and more. For example, the police would have more limitations on when they could pull people over or conduct stop and frisks. If one officer saw another breaking the rules, they would be required to intervene and could be punished if they didn't. And the MPD would have to post a public notice and a draft of policy changes online in several languages to inform the community.

In March 2023 the Minneapolis City Council unanimously approved the agreement and a four-year plan to carry it out. They plan to hire an independent evaluator to oversee the reform. But the agreement must first go to the Hennepin County District Court for a judge to accept and enforce it. Many city council members celebrated the agreement but noted it was only the first step of local police reform.

The Department of Justice also investigated whether the MPD had violated federal law and the US Constitution, releasing an eighty-nine-page report Friday, June 16, 2023, that called for reform of the department. The report found that MPD did have a pattern of violating the rights of Black and Native American people, and the Department of Justice and the Minnesota Department of Human Rights will agree to a federal consent decree based on the findings.

A protester carries a sign saying, "Abolish the police," at a Black Lives Matter rally in Washington, DC, in August 2020.

ABOLISH THE POLICE

Abolition is an idea that goes further than defunding or disbanding police. It suggests completely eliminating law enforcement agencies. Similar to defunding, the resources used to fund police departments would be, instead, used to establish and support community services that treat the underlying systemic issues that lead to crime. For example, funding could be used to provide mental health clinics to address mental illness and crises, food shelves to eliminate hunger, and job training centers to address unemployment. Abolitionists seek to create a community network that can address both daily and systemic challenges. Daily challenges are issues impacting the quality of life of community members related to overall safety and well-being. Systemic challenges include addressing homelessness instead of charging someone with a crime such as panhandling or loitering

LEADER IN THE ABOLITIONIST MOVEMENT

Angela Davis is a scholar, professor, political activist, and abolitionist. She was a member of the Black Panthers and gained national attention in 1970 when she was charged with murder, kidnapping, and conspiracy in connection with a courthouse incident in California. She became a symbol of resistance

Angela Davis at Oregon State University, 2019

against racial injustice and state repression, with her case attracting widespread support and sparking an international campaign for her freedom. After over a year in prison, Davis was acquitted of all charges in 1972 and has become one of the most prominent voices of the abolitionist movement. Davis has advocated for the abolishment of prisons and the criminal justice system. She is a cofounder of Critical Resistance, a national group that seeks to bring social change through three key strategic actions: dismantling policing systems and imprisonment, changing perspective, and building partnerships for change.

Davis analyzed the societal context that leads to violence and crime and challenged the idea that crime prevention should focus solely on penalizing the offender or perpetrator of violence. Alternatively, the community would address the conditions that lead to the crime. She shares her vision of abolitionism in her books, *Are Prisons Obsolete?* and *Freedom Is a Constant Struggle*.

"Because abolition is not just about changing institutions, it's about changing people's ideas, it's about changing prevailing ideology."

—Angela Davis

A CHANGE IN SOCIETY

The following words are from activist and organizer Mariame Kaba's book *We Do This 'Til We Free Us: Abolitionist Organizing and Transforming Justice*.

> People like me who want to abolish prisons and police, however, have a vision of a different society, built on cooperation instead of individualism, on mutual aid instead of self-preservation. What would the country look like if it had billions of extra dollars to spend on housing, food, and education for all? This change in society wouldn't happen immediately, but the protests show that many people are ready to embrace a different vision of safety and justice.
>
> When the streets calm and people suggest once again that we hire more Black police officers or create more civilian review boards, I hope that we remember all the times those efforts have failed.

(standing around), and providing mental health support instead of criminalizing behavior associated with a mental health condition.

Abolitionism explores crime through a restorative approach, drawing upon the principles of restorative justice. Crime is characterized as a community challenge, and neighbors, business owners, and other community members have a shared responsibility to address the harm caused, restore harmony, and bring healing for all parties. For example, when a property is damaged, such as by graffiti on a local office building, the three pillars of restorative justice are implemented: 1) harm and need (addressing the impact on the business owner and community), 2) obligation (the offender taking responsibility to make things right), and 3) engagement (creating ways to prevent this type of behavior in the future).

Abolition is not something that could happen overnight. It requires a process of reflection, engagement, and action. Countries such as Northern Ireland and the Republic of Georgia have embarked on this journey. Northern Ireland developed an independent commission to address concerns about the police force, the Royal Ulster Constabulary (RUC). RUC was highly militarized and not representative of the community it served. The community was primarily Catholic and experienced high rates of mistreatment at the hands of the police. In 1998 the country brought together an independent commission to address concerns about policing and develop recommendations for change. The findings of these efforts were compiled into a report called the Patten Report and led to the creation of a new police force, the Police Service of Northern Ireland, that replaced RUC in 2001.

The Republic of Georgia experienced a lack of public trust in law enforcement due to police corruption and abuse. In 2004 the new president Mikheil Saakashvili decided to take action by dissolving the Ministry of Internal Affairs. The Traffic Police was disbanded and every officer was fired. They were replaced with a new police force, the Patrol Police. These officers had no previous training in law enforcement, which offered a fresh start in ending previous patterns of corruption. The agency focuses on building positive relationships with the public and fostering trust through regular interaction and engagement, including initiatives such as community policing programs, public awareness campaigns, and community outreach activities. Its community-oriented approach and commitment to public service contributes to its positive reputation both domestically and internationally.

In the US, there are policy implications related to how to dismantle a police force and reallocate resources from police budgets to other community priorities. Some police departments are written into city law so laws and policies would have to be changed. While others will have to dramatically shift their budgets and transform their current model of public safety. And preparation has to be made to fill gaps in community services. It takes a community-wide commitment to change by investing in education, economic development, and a culture of health. Abolition requires people to look for and create new solutions. It does not look at policing as the only solution when a crime occurs.

Public Health

In some communities, a focus on a Culture of Health framework led by the Robert Wood Johnson Foundation has supported the health and wellness of the entire community, neighbors, and law enforcement alike. Communities across the nation face barriers to accessing health care, combating environmental justice, and increasing access to healthy foods by ending food deserts. In this type of community, "everyone has access to the care they need and a fair and just opportunity to make healthier choices. In a Culture of Health, communities flourish and individuals thrive." It recognizes that healthy communities are strong, safe, and welcoming.

In 2020 two things threatened the health and wellness of millions of people. The first was the COVID-19 pandemic. Due to racial disparities in preexisting health conditions, communities of color were experiencing coronavirus infections and deaths at a significantly higher rate than their white counterparts. The second public health issue was the impact of racial injustice brought to light following the murder of George Floyd in May 2020. It could no longer be denied that America had a challenge to solve and that systemic change was needed. The social tensions led to an explosion of rage. There was a call to action and unwillingness to wait any longer for justice and fairness no matter the color of one's skin.

Challenges such as a lack of access to healthy food or safe housing are active barriers to a healthy and vibrant community. In the United States, communities of color are suffering from a number of these challenges, which directly impact their health. For instance, Black children have a higher rate of diabetes. During COVID-19, the number of cases doubled. Children of color tend to live in neighborhoods with less access to quality food, limited recreational spaces for outdoor activities, and higher levels of violence, according to Darrell Hudson, a health disparities researcher at the University of Washington in Saint Louis. Black people are 13 percent of the general population in the US, but 21 percent of Black people live below the poverty line, and 40 percent of people who are unhoused are Black.

On April 8, 2021, the Centers for Disease Control and Prevention—an Atlanta, Georgia-based institution that oversees the nation's public health—declared racism a public health threat. Its director, Dr. Rochelle P. Walensky, acknowledged that

> "Change culture and you change lives. You can also change the course of history."
>
> —Resmaa Menakem, My Grandmother's Hands

Dr. Rochelle Walensky answers questions during a hearing to examine the 2022 budget request for the Centers for Disease Control and Prevention. Walensky and her team seek to address health concerns that are directly related to issues facing communities of color.

these structural issues are contributing to the health and economic challenges facing communities of color: "racism, discrimination, and historical disenfranchisement." Her team developed a plan to implement 150 commitments for change to promote racial equity and build healthy communities. The commitments include promoting maternal health, reducing birth defects, and addressing gendered racism and discrimination in the workplace.

Policing is high-stress work. Officers deal with and experience trauma and violence as part of their job. Some of their health problems include weight management. They have a higher obesity rate than the general public. Officers also have higher rates of stress-related sickness from heart disease to chronic pain. As a result, police have a shorter life span. They have a 55 percent chance of dying between the ages of fifty-five and sixty, in comparison to white males in the general public in the same age group where it is just 1 percent. Further, mental health challenges are often not addressed in police departments. Researchers have demonstrated the need for more counselors and peer support groups to support the health and wellness of officers, which would provide them with the tools to manage and address stress together as a community.

Police officers face violence while on duty. In 2021 seventy-three officers were killed in the United States, an increase from forty-six officers killed in 2020. Every five days, an officer is murdered. Many officers are concerned about the large number of guns on the streets. "There are more than 393 million civilian-owned firearms in the United States, or enough for every man, woman and child to own one and still have 67 million guns left over." The United States makes up about only 4 percent of the world's population.

THE IMPACT OF POLICE KILLINGS

Communities of color experience stress and trauma related to police killings of unarmed Black Americans. It has a ripple effect across the community as individuals experience loss and grief. These police killings could lead to fifty-five million more poor mental health days each year, according to research from the Perelman School of Medicine at the University of Pennsylvania and the Boston University School of Public Health.

Overall, daily experiences of racial discrimination lead to greater health risks due to stress. Research found one in four or five Black Americans experiences some type of discrimination at least once a week.

Community engagement officer Raphael Rockwell (*left*) listens to a speaker during a class on de-escalating tactics and avoiding the use of force in San Francisco.

Yet, Americans own nearly 46 percent of the world's civilian-owned guns.

In some countries such as Norway, Ireland, and Malawi, the police do not carry guns. Police use other methods to address conflict. While in some countries such as Cambodia and Vatican City/Holy See, it is prohibited for civilians to own guns. Other countries such as Japan have restrictive gun laws.

In the US, the high number of civilians with guns poses a safety risk when officers are working in the community. Community groups, public health groups, and police departments work together to address this issue through education by raising awareness about the impact of gun violence and hosting gun buyback programs. The buyback programs are a unified effort to get guns off the street.

Reimagining Public Safety

Many people feel that America's current vision of public safety is not working and that finding the solution requires input from all members of a community—police, government officials, health-care providers, advocates, business owners, educators, and neighbors.

With this vision for the future, public safety can no longer be characterized as solely the role of the police. The current societal challenges require the engagement of all of us. Everyone has a role to play in building safe communities. Police, government, health-care providers, business owners, and neighbors must work together to improve the quality of life, ensure the prosperity of the community, and strive toward equity and justice.

"It's organising. It's the work. And if people continue to do that work, and continue to organise against racism and provide new ways of thinking about how to transform our respective societies, that is what will make the difference."

—Angela Davis

Armand Coleman (*left*), executive director of the Transformational Prison Project (TPP), talks with a former prisoner. TPP is a restorative justice organization that focuses on dialogue and bringing together to share their stories of trauma.

CHAPTER 5

BUILDING STRONG AND SAFE COMMUNITIES

It is often said that "we can't arrest our way out of a problem." This statement acknowledges that getting tough on crime cannot heal racial injustice or solve the multifaceted challenges facing society. A new approach is needed that focuses on creating strong and safe communities rooted in racial equity. This approach combines both preventive measures that create a new pathway to the future and intervention strategies to address current challenges.

Restorative Justice

Another model for building community safety is restorative justice. This approach promotes healing and reconciliation after harm is done. Restorative justice focuses on the interrelatedness of the human experience and seeks to address the question of how to "make things right." In restorative justice, the emphasis is on addressing the needs of the victim, the offender, and the community affected by the offense. It recognizes that crime is not just a violation of laws but also a harm done to individuals and communities. The goal of restorative justice is to repair the harm after a crime has occurred. It focuses on three key pillars: harm experienced by individuals and the community, the offender's obligation to make things "right," and collective engagement in finding a solution.

"In a real sense all life is inter-related. All men are caught in an inescapable network of mutuality, tied in a single garment of destiny. Whatever affects one directly, affects all indirectly. I can never be what I ought to be until you are what you ought to be, and you can never be what you ought to be until I am what I ought to be. . . . This is the inter-related structure of reality."

—Martin Luther King Jr.

A community member can initiate restorative justice. It also can be offered as an alternative to the traditional legal system. The only requirement is that it is voluntary since the offender must acknowledge the harm and seek to work to address it. A facilitator guides the process. Restorative justice may occur in a circle, victim-offender mediation, or family group conferencing. Circles are commonly used, and there are different types of circles (talking, healing, listening, and community building). The circle can be used to reach goals and objectives from addressing a crime to managing conflicts in schools between students.

In a growing number of cities, restorative justice has become a key part of police officer training, including conflict management, community building, and de-escalation

HEALING FAMILIES AND COMMUNITIES THROUGH RESTORATIVE JUSTICE

In 2005 Mary Johnson founded From Death to Life, an organization based on restorative justice. She works to bring healing and reconciliation to families who have lost a loved one due to violence (victims) and those who caused harm (offenders). This mission is personal to her since her only child was murdered. On February 12, 1993, her twenty-year-old son Laramiun Byrd was killed by a sixteen-year-old, Oshea Israel, who was convicted of second-degree murder and sentenced to twenty-five years in prison. Mary decided to forgive Oshea and visited him while he was in prison. They built a bond, and she refers to him as her "spiritual son." He was since released from prison, and the pair work together to share their story of healing.

RESTORATIVE JUSTICE IN ACTION

Examples of how restorative justice can support public safety and community building include these:

- **Reduce juvenile crime.** In England and Scotland, "accountability conferencing" has been used to help juveniles understand the impact of criminal behavior on communities. Juveniles are required to perform acts of restitution in the community, such as repairing damaged property, mentoring elementary students, and performing community service.

- **Address racial disparities in the incarceration rates.** The Summit-University Frogtown Community Circle was founded in Saint Paul, Minnesota, to minister to the needs of Black male offenders. The circle took a holistic approach by reintegrating offenders into the community impacted by crime and violence.

- **Remedy conflict in schools.** Student-led circles have been used to handle school disruption and minimize bullying. Fellow students play an active role in resolving the conflict. Students develop the necessary tools to address conflict and develop tools to manage conflict in the future.

strategies. Leveraging the principles of restorative justice, officers work with community members to create safe communities and prevent crime. Restorative justice strategies acknowledge that crime does not just impact an individual but negatively affects an entire community. Through this collaboration, community and police relations improved, communities restored broken bonds, and mutual respect has been established.

Prevention

As repeated studies have shown, addressing crime requires addressing human needs. Building an equitable vision of public safety combines both prevention and intervention. Prevention is related to the type of community initiatives that are meant to help people before they resort to criminal behavior. Intervention is meant to help reintegrate someone into the community after they have entered the criminal justice system.

BREAKING THE POVERTY CYCLE

In the United States, 37.2 million people live in poverty. When community members are unable to access food, housing, health care, employment, or educational opportunities, it creates vulnerability and leads to marginalization, which directly impacts public safety. What is the solution to addressing a social challenge of this magnitude? An investment in infrastructure and opportunities has been suggested. When Andy Cooke, a British police chief, was asked the question, What would he do with a £5 billion investment in law enforcement (over US$6 billion)? he did not focus on expanding his police department or hiring more officers. He said he would allocate only £1 billion to those needs and use the other £4 billion to invest in the community. "The best crime prevention is increased

> **"If we're really concerned about deterring crime, we should focus on the basic social services people need."**
>
> —*Rachel Gilmer, codirector of the Dream Defenders*

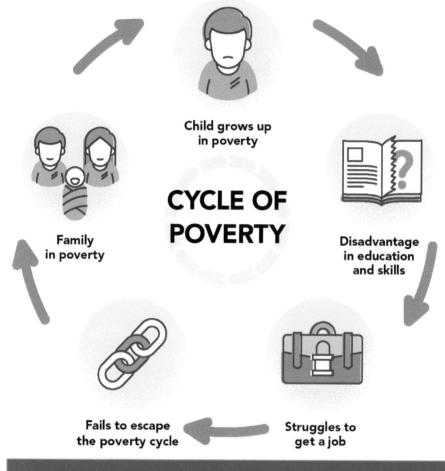

CYCLE OF POVERTY

Child grows up
in poverty

Disadvantage
in education
and skills

Struggles to
get a job

Fails to escape
the poverty cycle

Family
in poverty

This diagram shows how unemployment, lack of education, or chronic financial problems create a cycle of poverty.

opportunity and reduced poverty," Cooke said. "If you give [someone] a legal opportunity to actually earn money, a legal opportunity to actually have a good standard of living, a number of people would take that because they know . . . they don't have to worry."

MASLOW'S HIERARCHY OF NEEDS

Abraham Maslow was an American psychologist and professor at Brandeis University. In 1943 he developed a framework that outlines human needs in five categories: physiological (food, shelter, clothing), safety (job, health), love (friendship, belonging), esteem (positive self-image), and self-actualization (seeking to reach goals). When considering building safe and strong communities, Maslow's Hierarchy of Needs can be relevant in several ways:

Addressing basic needs. Ensuring that individuals' physiological needs, such as food, shelter, and health care, are met is crucial. By providing access to these basic needs, we can help prevent individuals from engaging in criminal activities driven by desperation or survival instincts.

Promoting safety and security. Safety is a fundamental aspect of community well-being. It involves creating safe environments free from violence, crime, and hazards. This includes effective law enforcement, emergency services, and infrastructure that promote physical safety. Meeting safety needs fosters a sense of security and allows individuals to engage fully in their community.

Supporting social needs. Building strong social connections within a community is essential for community safety. When individuals feel a sense of belonging, they are more likely to look out for one another and work together to promote safety.

Enhancing self-esteem. Community safety can be enhanced by promoting self-esteem and respect among community members. This involves valuing diversity, promoting inclusivity, and providing opportunities for personal growth and achievement. When individuals feel respected and have a positive self-image, they are more likely to contribute positively to the community.

Encouraging self-actualization. Creating an environment that supports the self-actualization of community members contributes to community safety. This means providing access to education, job opportunities, cultural and artistic activities, and spaces for personal development.

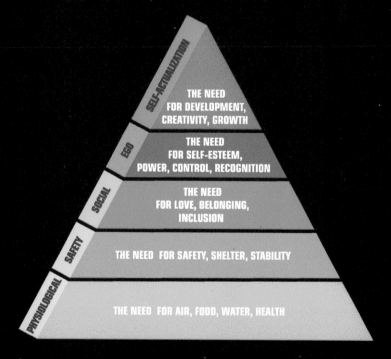

SELF-ACTUALIZATION

EGO

SOCIAL

SAFETY

PHYSIOLOGICAL

THE NEED FOR DEVELOPMENT, CREATIVITY, GROWTH

THE NEED FOR SELF-ESTEEM, POWER, CONTROL, RECOGNITION

THE NEED FOR LOVE, BELONGING, INCLUSION

THE NEED FOR SAFETY, SHELTER, STABILITY

THE NEED FOR AIR, FOOD, WATER, HEALTH

Alvin Irby (*right*), founder of Barbershop Books, along with professional football player Jarvis Jenkins show books to kids during a youth reading event in Harlem in 2016.

INCREASING LITERACY RATES

Research demonstrates a connection between illiteracy and future incarceration. Literacy levels among prisoners are considerably lower than the level of the general population, according to the National Adult Literacy Survey. One in four students in the United States—twenty-five million children—are not able to read. Students not proficient in reading by third grade are four times more likely to drop out of school. Dropouts are three and a half times more likely to be arrested or jailed for criminal activity. And 85 percent of children in the juvenile justice system and between 70 and 75 percent of the adult prison population are not literate. According to the US Department of Justice, "The link between academic failure and delinquency, violence, and crime is welded to reading failure."

Communities focused on literacy are developing initiatives to support literacy. Barbershop Books is one such organization that focuses on inspiring Black boys to read through their connections to a special community space: barbershops. This is important when more than 82 percent of Black male fourth-grade students have not become proficient in reading. This organization is providing Black boys with content that centers on the experiences of Black male characters and with role models who they meet at the barbershop.

Intervention

Typically, crime intervention begins with an arrest by a police officer and ends with a conviction of a crime. When an offender returns to the community, they face collateral consequences that pose a challenge to reentering society and finding stability. They enter a world with limited access to jobs, opportunities, and community connections.

As we reimagine public safety, experts are coming up with opportunities to disrupt cycles of incarceration and strengthen the community.

ALTERNATIVES TO DETENTION AND INCARCERATION

When someone is convicted of a crime, imprisonment tends to be the default punishment. But alternative community-based options are available. One example of an alternative is the Casey Foundation's Juvenile Detention Alternatives Initiative, which provides offending youth with community coaches and community-based centers for learning. These resources aid youth in finding the support of caring adults, developing basic life skills, and improving academic achievement. The initiative is a national model in forty states and the District of Columbia.

ESTABLISH SPECIALTY COURTS

Specialty courts address specific types of nonviolent offenses. Rather than sentencing a defendant to prison, a judge can have them participate in an intensive probation program focused on education and treatment. For example, a drug court requires defendants to attend rehabilitation and holds them accountable through regular court appearances and random drug testing. At the end of the program, charges may be dismissed or sentences may be reduced.

Another example is the peer court, which engages youth in problem-solving within their own community with other young people their age, promotes prosocial behavior, and fosters leadership development. It is an alternative to the traditional operations of the juvenile justice system, where youth (peer jurors) support their peer (offender) in addressing delinquent acts or other behavioral challenges. This type of diversion initiative places youth at the forefront of addressing challenges in their community while advancing the restorative justice goal of "making things right." The four potential benefits of the youth court model are 1) accountability (addressing the underlying harm), 2) timeliness (handled more expeditiously than the juvenile justice system), 3) cost savings (led by volunteers, hence limited costs to the community), and 4) community cohesion (respect for the law).

Youth court also promotes community building and supports the local economy. This is shown by the outcomes of the Time Dollar Youth Court. In this diversion program, youth are connected to the community and discover how they can be of service. They learn how to contribute to their community. "Community service allows youth to bring valuable contributions to the community, feel better about theirselves, and establish or rebuild broken relationships.

Jurors are actually expanding the rule of law, getting their peers to think about what is fair and just." Youth courts yield value to the community. In one year, youth completed 1,734,771 hours of service in their communities worth over $11 million in restitution through community service. This transforms a negative situation (youth causing harm and being referred to the juvenile justice system) into an enriching learning experience with positive outcomes. Youth are connected back to their communities through acts of service from volunteering at a local library to tutoring younger students.

"Community service allows youth to bring valuable contributions to the community, feel better about theirselves, and establish or rebuild broken relationships."

These specialty courts offer an opportunity for judges to provide additional resources and support to help offenders get their lives back on track. They serve as a valuable tool for addressing the root cause of crime and reducing recidivism, or repeat offenses.

SUPPORT SECOND CHANCES

Employment can be a tool for reducing recidivism and a return to prison. But finding a job can be difficult for people convicted of a crime. According to the American Civil Liberties Union, only 25 percent of formerly incarcerated individuals are employed a year after release. Providing job development resources for those exiting the prison system is one way communities can help them successfully reenter society. Homeboy Industries is one example of how community members can help. The international

Women prepare lunch at Homegirl Café in Los Angeles. Homegirl Café employs and trains thirty at-risk and formerly gang-involved young women in restaurant and catering work. Homegirl Café is a part of Homeboy Industries.

program supports reentry and reintegration for offenders and gang-involved individuals through job skills training and by providing services such as General Educational Development (GED) test prep and tattoo removal. A GED expands educational opportunities, which helps to open doors for future careers. Tattoo removal can help to reduce stereotypes and biases against people who have a criminal record. Father Gregory Boyle, the founder of Homeboy Industries, seeks to create stronger communities by bringing people together. This recognizes that everyone has value and can make a valuable contribution to society. He challenges the stereotype that having a criminal record diminishes your self-worth and dignity. He raises the question of whether a person should be judged based upon the worst thing they have ever done.

Reimagining the future of public safety is an opportunity to create and implement new strategies for both crime prevention and community building. This extends beyond a policing model or community initiative. Instead, it focuses on how to minister to the needs of community members. Models that focus on health and wellness and restorative practices as a way of life can add new dimensions to public safety. These models aid in creating unity and harmony in the community. Other tools include ensuring people have stable housing since shelter is the foundation of meeting one's basic needs. Families with stable housing can find stability and thrive. A combination of prevention and intervention strategies can provide valuable tools to address crime and build strong and safe communities.

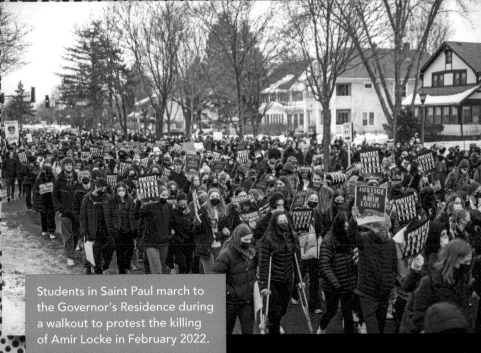

Students in Saint Paul march to the Governor's Residence during a walkout to protest the killing of Amir Locke in February 2022.

CHAPTER 6

GETTING INVOLVED

Now is the accepted time, not tomorrow, not some more convenient season. It is today that our best work can be done and not some future day or future year.
—*W. E. B. Du Bois, author, historian, Pan-Africanism scholar*

Young people can and have been at the forefront of the movement to reimagine policing by pointing out the many ways to get involved in building a stronger and safer community, both big and small. You, too, can help to lead change in your community and demonstrate the type of leadership needed to make a difference. Let's explore a few key leadership strategies.

A Call to Leadership

Leadership is often characterized as a position or title. Someone may be described as a leader because they exercise power over others. Redefining leadership as a tool for how we can each make a difference in our community is key to reimagining public safety. Age restrictions don't apply. You are never too young or too old to lead social change. The opportunity to make an impact is within your reach.

Leaders are willing to pause, reflect, and grow. And leadership is a journey, not a destination. It is a lifelong commitment to learning and exploration.

Leadership begins with exploring: What is in your hands to make a difference in the world? Power and influence lie within your hands. You have the transformative power to address social justice challenges. You can look beyond race, culture, or creed (beliefs) to work with others to leave the world a better place.

Leaders Help to Build a Vision for Racial Justice

The United States is increasingly racially diverse, so promoting inclusion is key. Developing the skills needed to promote inclusion is the job of everyone whether you are a police

"Freedom is people realizing they are their own leaders."

—Diane Nash, a founding member of the Student Nonviolent Coordinating Committee

Los Angeles high school students, teachers, and law enforcement officers walk across the Sixth Street Viaduct as part of the third annual Good Trouble Walk & Cultural Sensitivity Summit in 2023.

officer, judge, doctor, engineer, or young leader. You can support inclusion by understanding how the cultural landscape is changing and making a commitment to building anti-racist communities. Soon America will no longer have an ethnic majority—no one ethnic group will account for over 50 percent of the population. Researchers predict that this will happen by 2044. Over half of the 19.6 million children under the age of five are children of color, and most new births are children of color.

This should be a moment to celebrate. Yet we still need to move from diversity to inclusion. Diversity looks at the representation of individuals in a particular setting whether at school or in the community. Inclusion focuses on building the type of communities where everyone can succeed and thrive.

To achieve this goal of inclusion, we need to build a vision for racial justice. This starts with a commitment to becoming anti-racist, to dare to speak up and stand up against racism. Becoming anti-racist is a commitment to learning about the history of race and finding ways to combat racism. According to educator and author of *This Book Is Antiracist* Tiffany Jewell, "Racism is personal prejudice and bias and the systemic misuse and abuse of power by institutions." An anti-racist is also committed to taking action to address racism and building a community rooted in our shared humanity and common destiny.

Research has shown that there is no biological or scientific basis for classifying individuals into racial categories. This includes defining the concept of race, which classifies individuals in a caste system based on their physical attributes. Race has been used to justify slavery and uphold principles of white supremacy. Yet DNA shows that the genetic makeup of humanity has many similarities and is fundamentally the same no matter the color of your skin.

"Race, as we currently carry such a notion in our heads, is largely a myth, a fiction, or a stage of false consciousness."

—Mahmoud El-Kati, history professor and author

By learning more about the history of race and taking a stand against racism, you can be an effective leader. You will gain the understanding to address biases, stereotypes, and prejudices. And you will develop the skills to address the racial disparities in policing and the administration of justice.

Leaders Embrace Restorative Justice as a Way of Life

Leaders build new community connections and serve as lead problem solvers. Restorative justice provides key tools for reaching these goals. The main focus is addressing the question of how to make things right.

Seeking to make things right may be addressing a challenge at school or helping to end a dispute among friends. For instance, in the criminal justice context, this may be participating in a youth peer court after a school fight. Peer court provides an opportunity to make things right by holding the offender accountable for the harm, providing the victim an opportunity to be heard, and drawing everyone together as a community to create a pathway forward. Restorative justice supports community building and peacemaking.

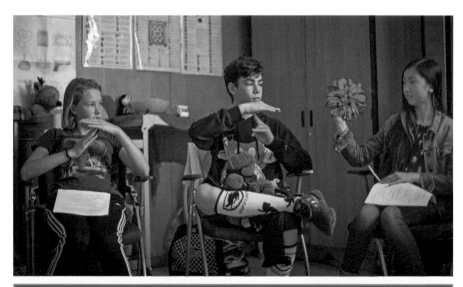

Students at Edna Brewer Middle School in Oakland participate in a restorative justice program in 2019.

"Ultimately, restorative justice signifies the dawning of a new justice, a Bright Sun, that transcends the punitive and narrow assumptions of prevailing justice and offers a broader view of justice inspired by indigenous values. That is, a new but old justice that is healing, relational, community-based, inclusivist, participatory, needs- and accountability-based, and forward-looking."

—Fania Davis, founding director of
Restorative Justice for Oakland Youth

Leaders Seek to Educate Themselves and Others

As a leader, learn more about laws and rights in your area. Educate yourself and educate others. Read about racial bias and other issues in policing and criminal justice, either nationally, locally, or both. You may want to learn more about policing in schools or what reforms your police department has enacted already. Talk to family, friends, neighbors, teachers, police officers, government officials, and other community members to understand their perspectives on the issues and to share what you have learned.

One place to start is reading the Constitution and Bill of Rights. You can also take a basic civics course at school or through your community education program, and then share what you are learning about the importance of protecting basic liberties for all with your friends and community. Start with the promise of equality outlined in the Declaration of Independence. Our forefathers laid a foundation for our nation built on the values of justice and freedom.

The Bill of Rights, the first ten amendments to the Constitution, offers additional rights to citizens. Three specific amendments protect your rights during a police encounter. Familiarize yourself with the Fourth, Fifth, and Sixth Amendments, which protect citizens' rights through the criminal justice system.

The Fourth Amendment prohibits unlawful search and seizure:

> The right of the people to be secure in their persons, houses, papers, and effects, against unreasonable searches and seizures, shall not be violated, and no Warrants shall issue, but upon probable cause, supported by Oath or affirmation, and particularly describing the place to be searched, and the persons or things to be seized.

The Fifth Amendment outlines the right to be free from double jeopardy (charged for the same offense twice) and self-incrimination (the right to not testify against yourself):

> No person shall be held to answer for a capital, or otherwise infamous crime, unless on a presentment or indictment of a Grand Jury, except in cases arising in the land or naval forces, or in the Militia, when in actual service in time of War or public danger; nor shall any person be subject for the same offence to be twice put in jeopardy of life or limb; nor shall be compelled in any criminal case to be a witness against himself, nor be deprived of life, liberty, or property, without due process of law; nor shall private property be taken for public use, without just compensation.

UNDERSTANDING MIRANDA RIGHTS

In TV shows and movies, you may see a police officer reading a potential suspect the Miranda warning, which outlines that person's legal rights while in custody. This warning comes from a 1966 case: *Miranda v. Arizona*. Ernesto Miranda was arrested for rape and murder. Police officers in Miranda's hometown of Phoenix, where the crimes were committed, interrogated him. But the officers did not give him clear instructions that his Fifth Amendment right would allow him to remain silent. Nor did they inform him of his right to have an attorney with him as he faced questioning. Miranda eventually signed a written confession and was convicted of the crime based on that confession. The US Supreme Court overturned his conviction because the confession was not actually voluntary because he had no counsel and didn't fully understand what was happening to him. He was retried in Arizona, in 1967, and because his original confession could no longer be used as evidence, it was not presented at trial. Other evidence led to his conviction.

The statement police read to suspects during interrogations is the Miranda warning. It spells out five key rights:

- You have the right to remain silent.

- Anything you say can and will be used against you in a court of law.

- You have the right to speak to an attorney.

- If you cannot afford an attorney, one will be provided for you.

- Do you understand these rights I have just read to you?

The Sixth Amendment provides the right to a speedy trial and a jury trial:

> In all criminal prosecutions, the accused shall enjoy the right to a speedy and public trial, by an impartial jury of the State and district wherein the crime shall have been committed, which district shall have been previously ascertained by law, and to be informed of the nature and cause of the accusation; to be confronted with the witnesses against him; to have compulsory process for obtaining witnesses in his favor, and to have the Assistance of Counsel for his defence.

Leaders Take Action

In addition to being informed about your rights, you need to engage in your community. Change happens through persistent, organized efforts. A collective vision for the future is the guiding light. What is your vision for public safety in your community? What steps should be taken to achieve these goals?

Young people across the nation are organizing for change. They are outlining ways to prevent crime and strengthen their

"When people collectively come together and strategize and plan, working together and acting together, they create a power that they can effectively use in their situation to effect change."

—*James Lawson Jr., civil rights leader*

Professor Bob Brzenchek (*center*) and Pennsylvania State Police trooper Deanna Piekanski (*right*) present criminal justice major Elijah Demosthene with a certificate marking his completion of the Pennsylvania State Police Citizens Police Academy.

communities. This could include investing in social services to meet the basic needs of community members such as access to housing and food or even providing more resources in schools such as guidance counselors and vocational training.

Another way to get involved in the community is by serving in citizen academies and cadet programs to learn more about public safety. These programs tend to be available through your local police department. You can gain the tools to create change in your community while exploring careers in law enforcement and other criminal justice areas. You can attend career workshops at your school and conduct a job shadow or check out a career-related book at your library.

YOUTH LEADING CHANGE

The Citywide Youth Coalition focuses on supporting youth as they build the power needed to radically transform systems. The New Haven, Connecticut-based coalition was established as a nonprofit in 1994. Youth are trained in anti-racist education and youth leadership development. This training is based on the anti-racist principles of the People's Institute for Survival and Beyond: analyzing power, developing leadership, transforming gatekeeping, identifying and analyzing manifestation of racism, learning from history, maintaining accountability, building a network of support, sharing culture, and undoing internalized racial oppression, superiority, and inferiority.

The youth decided to list demands about policing issues. This included cutting the police budget and reinvesting in public schools and affordable housing and ensuring the community is involved with selecting members of the civilian review board. Civilian review boards investigate reports of police misconduct and make a recommendation to the police chief for further action.

Democracy is a crucial piece to the future of public safety. Another way to learn more about civic engagement is by training and serving as election judges. Serving as an election judge is a key opportunity to support elections and participate in democracy building. In many states, you can serve starting at sixteen years old.

Leaders Advocate for Change

Leaders recognize the power of writing for justice as a valuable tool of advocacy. You can write a letter to your representatives asking them to support police reform legislation or community programming. These representatives can be members of the city parks board, a city council, a school board, or county, state, or national governments. You can share your ideas about what the future of public safety should look like to help elected officials reimagine the future of public safety.

Your advocacy can also include the strategies of nonviolent resistance. Peaceful demonstration is a key method activists use to build solidarity and place pressure on decision-makers to address concerns. Protests across the nation have shaped policing policies and procedures. They have addressed such issues as banning choke holds and releasing body camera footage.

Boycotts are also used for advocacy. This focuses on the power of not spending your money at a certain place. For example, during the civil rights movement, the Black community organized and did not purchase goods from businesses that had discriminatory hiring practices. This was called the "Don't buy where you cannot work" campaign. The same methods are used today as people choose not to do business with organizations that support private prisons.

Public safety is key to the future of a more prosperous and vibrant United States. It seeks to ensure equal rights and justice. Policing is one component of public safety that can obtain this collective vision, and it will require strategic action and community engagement.

Strategic action and policy reform are needed to achieve this vision. This is a call to leadership—an invitation for you to use your voice to create change in your community.

THE TIME IS NOW

'm truly exhausted, but when I think back on the giants that
fought like the late John Lewis, Rosa Parks, Martin Luther King,
Harriet Tubman. All of those folks, I have no excuse.

—Tiffany Crutcher, sister of Terence Crutcher,
who was killed in 2016 by a police officer

Leading social change is like a relay race. The baton is passed
from one generation to the next. The abolitionists who fought
to end slavery carried the baton to the Reconstruction era.
They worked to eliminate slave patrols and ensure equal
rights. Civil rights leaders, young and old, fought to bury
Jim Crow laws and all forms of racial discrimination. During
the civil rights movement, Malcolm X, Martin Luther King
Jr., John Lewis, and young activists were determined to end
police brutality and racial terrorism. In 2013 three activists
created a hashtag with a unifying call to honor the human
dignity of all lives while addressing the urgent need to protect
Black lives from police violence. Across the world, "Black
Lives Matter" was chanted in unison to honor the lives of
unarmed Black men such as Terence Crutcher, George Floyd,
and others who were killed by the police. It is your turn to
lead change by reimagining public safety. How will you help
to build safe, strong, and vibrant communities where justice
reigns supreme?

GLOSSARY

abolitionist: someone who is dedicated to ending an institution, such as slavery or policing

advocate: someone who supports or promotes a cause or the interests of a particular group

collateral consequence: barriers and restrictions impacting people with a criminal record

defund: redirecting funding from policing to other community-based programs

disband: breaking up or dissolving an organization

disproportionate impact: when a policy impacts a certain group at a higher rate than others

excessive force: force beyond what is needed to address a situation

hot spot policing: using technology to address patterns in crime

inclusion: the act of including and accommodating people who have historically been marginalized due to their race, gender, sexuality, or ability

institutional racism: racism embedded with laws, policies, and regulations

intelligence-led policing: a policing model based on data and research

Jim Crow laws: laws after post-Reconstruction to deprive Black people of their rights

justice: fair treatment under the law

mass incarceration: refers to the United States having the highest number of people imprisoned in the world

Miranda warning: a warning given by police when someone is detained

misdemeanor: a minor crime or penalty that requires less than a year of imprisonment

order maintenance policing: policing that involves managing minor offenses and disorders to address community problems

police brutality: excessive force used by a police officer

policy: rules, laws, regulations, and procedures developed by the government

procedural justice: fairness and equity in administering justice

public safety: protection of the general public

racism: the belief that racial differences produce an inherent superiority of a particular race

Reconstruction: a period after the Civil War when attempts were made to address racial inequalities

reform: changing an organization or process

rehabilitation: providing training, education, and resources to improve the well-being of someone convicted of a crime

restorative justice: an approach to justice that focuses on repairing harm caused by an offense by recognizing harms and needs, seeking to right the wrong, and engaging those impacted

sanctity of life: a philosophy focused on a duty to protect human life and only use the amount of force necessary to achieve specified lawful goals

slave patrol: an organized group of armed citizens who controlled and oversaw the actions of enslaved individuals

social justice: equal political, social, and economic rights and opportunities

solidarity: unity in advancing a shared purpose and goals

stop and frisk: stopping someone who is suspected of committing a crime and patting them down to search for weapons or other illegal items

War on Drugs: national effort started by President Nixon in 1971 to address illegal drug use and drug trade by increasing enforcement by law enforcement and penalties for drug-related crimes

white supremacy: the belief that white people are superior and should have control over people of other races

SOURCE NOTES

12 "It's important for . . . this particular vulnerability.": Jordyn Phelps, "8 Powerful Quotes from President Obama's ABC Town Hall," ABC News, July 14, 2016, https://abcnews.go.com /Politics/powerful-quotes-president-obamas-abc-town-hall /story?id=40591539.

12 "eradicate white supremacy . . . state and vigilantes": "About," Black Lives Matter, accessed November 19, 2022, https:// blacklivesmatter.com/about.

17 "The police are . . . welfare and existence.": "Sir Robert Peel's Policing Principles," Law Enforcement Action Partnership, accessed January 24, 2023, https:// lawenforcementactionpartnership.org/peel-policing-principles.

24 "The basic mission . . . dealing with it.": "Sir Robert Peel's Nine Principles of Policing," *New York Times*, April 16, 2014, https:// www.nytimes.com/2014/04/16/nyregion/sir-robert-peels-nine -principles-of-policing.html.

29 "public enemy number one": Richard Nixon, "Remarks about an Intensified Program for Drug Abuse Prevention and Control," speech, press conference, White House Briefing Room, Washington, DC, June 17, 1971, https://www.presidency.ucsb .edu/documents/remarks-about-intensified-program-for-drug -abuse-prevention-and-control.

34 "On my honor . . . agency I serve": "Law Enforcement Oath of Honor," International Association of Chiefs of Police, accessed January 22, 2022, https://www.theiacp.org/sites/default/files /2021-01/246910_IACP_Oath_of_Honor_11x8.5_p1%20%281%29 .pdf.

37 "except as a . . . been duly convicted.": U.S. Const. amend. XIII, § 1.

40 "The common goal . . . recognized as humans.": Malcolm X, "'Racism: The Cancer that Is Destroying America' — *Egyptian Gazette* (August 25,1964)," available online at Complete Malcolm X, last modified April 29, 2023, https://malcolmxfiles .com/collection/racism-the-cancer-that-is-destroying-america -egyptian-gazette-cairo-egypt-august-25-1964/.

43   "Nonviolence is a . . . will eventually win.": "Six Principles of Nonviolence," Martin Luther King, Jr. Research and Education Institute, accessed February 28, 2023, https://kinginstitute .stanford.edu/sites/mlk/files/lesson-activities/six_principles _of_nonviolence.pdf.

47   "police the police": Gabriel H. Sanchez, "These Pictures Show the Impact of the Black Panthers on America," BuzzFeed News, February 13, 2020, https://www.buzzfeednews.com/article /gabrielsanchez/black-panthers-huey-newton-bobby-seale -police-brutality.

48   "Some people say . . . racism with solidarity.": Fred Hampton, "Power Anywhere Where There's People," speech, Olivet Church, Chicago, 1969, https://www.historyisaweapon.com /defcon1/fhamptonspeech.html.

49   "long, hot summer of 1967": Ramtin Arablouei and Rund Abdelfatah, "The Long Hot Summer," *Throughline*, produced by NPR, podcast, July 9, 2020, https://www.npr.org/transcripts /888184490.

49   "The chaos that . . . 3,500 people arrested.": Morgan Jerkins, "She Played a Key Role in the Police Response to the Watts Riots. The Memory Still Haunts Her—But Black History Is Full of Haunting Memories," *Time*, August 3, 2020, https://time.com /5873228/watts-riots-memory.

50   "What happened? Why . . . again and again?": National Advisory Commission on Civil Disorders, *Kerner Commission, Report of the National Commission on Civil Disorders* (Washington, DC: US Government Printing Office, 1968), 18, https://belonging .berkeley.edu/sites/default/files/kerner_commission_full_report .pdf?file=1&force=1.

50   "moving toward two . . . of every American": National Advisory Commission on Civil Disorders.

51   "First level of . . . inadequate welfare programs": National Advisory Commission on Civil Disorders.

52   "accounted for 15% . . . arrests in [2016].": "Report to the United Nations on Racial Disparities in the U.S. Criminal Justice System," Sentencing Project, April 19, 2018, https://www .sentencingproject.org/reports/report-to-the-united-nations -on-racial-disparities-in-the-u-s-criminal-justice-system.

53   "African-American adults are . . . times as likely.": "Report to the United Nations."

54   "More than one . . . usage was comparable.": "Report to the United Nations."

57   "I am not . . . away with murder.": Tadd Haislop, "Colin Kaepernick Kneeling Timeline: How Protests during the National Anthem Started a Movement in the NFL," *Sporting News*, September 13, 2020, https://www.sportingnews.com/us/nfl /news/colin-kaepernick-kneeling-protest-timeline /xktu6ka4diva1s5jxaylrcsse.

59–60 "Native Americans are . . . by law enforcement.": "A System Constructed to Fail Us All," Lakota People's Law Project, July 10, 2020, https://lakotalaw.org/news/2020-07-10/native-lives-matter -2020.

61   "From the arrival . . . their own hands.": Angela Davis, *Policing the Black Man: Arrest, Prosecution, and Imprisonment* (New York: Pantheon Books, 2017), xii.

66   "Why are we . . . officers like soldiers?": German Lopez, "Trump's Plan to Give Police Easier Access to Military Weapons, Explained," Vox, August 28, 2017, https://www.vox.com/policy -and-politics/2017/8/28/16214600/trump-police-military-sessions.

67–68 "The broken-windows theory . . . cause, of crime.": Alex S. Vitale, *The End of Policing* (New York: Verso, 2021), 7.

68   "How do we ensure . . . this important question.": Shankar Vedantam et al., "How a Theory of Crime and Policing Was Born, and Went Terribly Wrong," NPR, November 1, 2016, https://www .npr.org/2016/11/01/500104506/broken-windows-policing -and-the-origins-of-stop-and-frisk-and-how-it-went-wrong.

69   "a collaborative law . . . enhanced intelligence operations.":
Rich LeCates, "Intelligence-Led Policing: Changing the Face of
Crime Prevention," *Police Chief*, October 17, 2018, https://www
.policechiefmagazine.org/changing-the-face-crime-prevention.

73   "Community policing is . . . fear of crime.": The Office of
Community Oriented Policing Services, *Community Policing
Defined* (Washington, DC: US Department of Justice, 2012), 1.

75   "We are Oscar Grant.": Leslie Fulbright et al., "BART Protesters
in SF: 'We Are Oscar Grant!'" SFGATE, January 13, 2009, https://
www.sfgate.com/bayarea/article/BART-protesters-in-SF-We-are
-Oscar-Grant-3254646.php.

77   "I can't breathe.": "'I Can't Breathe': Eric Garner Put in
Chokehold by NYPD Officer—Video," video, 1:30, posted by
Guardian (US edition), December 4, 2014, https://www
.theguardian.com/us-news/video/2014/dec/04/i-cant-breathe
-eric-garner-chokehold-death-video.

77   "neighborhood peacemaker": History.com editors, "Eric Garner
Dies in NYPD Chokehold," History, July 17, 2014, https://www
.history.com/this-day-in-history/eric-garner-dies-nypd
-chokehold.

77   "Every time you . . . it stops today.": "'I Can't Breathe': Eric
Garner Put in Chokehold by NYPD Officer—Video," 0:44.

79   "Thou shalt not kill": Fiza Pirani, "What Is the Silent Parade?
Remembering the Iconic 1917 Civil Rights March," *Atlanta
Journal-Constitution*, July 26, 2019, https://www.ajc.com/news
/local/what-the-silent-parade-google-honors-iconic-1917-civil
-rights-march/giuC6SvZjq0qjHgyshh6bO.

79   "We have a . . . to do something.": Morgan Brinlee, "8 Incredible
John Lewis Quotes," Bustle, January 14, 2017, https://www
.bustle.com/p/these-john-lewis-quotes-about-justice-civil-rights
-are-the-perfect-example-of-how-words-become-action-30445.

79   "Black lives matter.": Jelani Cobb, "The Matter of Black Lives,"
New Yorker, March 6, 2016, https://www.newyorker.com
/magazine /2016/03/14/where-is-black-lives-matter-headed.

80   "black people. I . . . Our lives matter.": Cobb.

80   "freedom, liberation . . . justice": "Home: Black Lives Matter,"
      Black Lives Matter, accessed January 24, 2023, https://
      blacklivesmatter.com.

85   "all law enforcement . . . applying deadly force.": Office of
      Minnesota Attorney General Keith Ellison, "Pohland Family
      Foundation to Fund Recommendations for Reducing Police-
      Involved Deadly-Force Encounters," news release February 25,
      2021, https://www.ag.state.mn.us/Office/Communications
      /2021/02/25_PohlandFamilyFoundation.asp.

86   "Establish a formal . . . to review outcomes.": State of
      Minnesota Working Group on Police-Involved Deadly Force
      Encounters, "Working Group on Police-Involved Deadly Force
      Encounters Recommendations and Action Steps," Working
      Group on Police-Involved Deadly Force Encounters, Minnesota
      Department of Public Safety, February 2020, https://dps
      .mn.gov/divisions/co/working-group/Documents/police
      -involved-deadly-force-encounters-recommendations.pdf.

86   "[D]iscuss strategies to . . . Enforcement Officer's request.":
      State of Minnesota Working Group on Police-Involved Deadly
      Force Encounters.

93   "there's a mobile . . . path to recovery.": Minyvonne Burke,
      "Policing Mental Health: Recent Deaths Highlight Concerns over
      Officer Response," NBC News, May 16, 2021, https://www
      .nbcnews.com/news/us-news/policing-mental-health-recent
      -deaths-highlight-concerns-over-officer-response-n1266935.

95   "I'm tired. I'm . . . from being tired.": Lauren Hirsch, "George
      Floyd's Brother Testifies before Congress: 'Stop the Pain,'"
      CNBC, last updated June 10, 2020, https://www.cnbc.com
      /2020/06/10/george-floyd-brother-tells-congress-stop-the-pain
      .html.

97   "crime cannot be . . . and individual citizens.": President's
      Commission on Law Enforcement and Administration of Justice,
      The Challenge of Crime in a Free Society (Washington, DC: US
      Government Printing Office, 1967), v.

99 "defunding a system . . . a consistent basis.": Malaika Jabali, "Do Cops Make Us Safe?," *Essence*, last updated August 11, 2021, https://www.essence.com/news/do-cops-make-us-safe.

99 "It's time for . . . and poor Chicagoans.": Daniel La Spata et al., "Cutting Funding for Police Could Lead to a Better and Safer Chicago," *Chicago Sun-Times*, June 8, 2020, https://chicago .suntimes.com/2020/6/8/21284037/chicago-police-department -unfunding-cpd-city-council-budget.

99 "criminalizing mental illness": Wendy Glauser, "Why Some Doctors Want to Defund the Police," *Canadian Medical Association Journal* 192, no. 48 (2020): 1664–1665, https://doi .org/10.1503/cmaj.1095905.

101 "We were going . . . and not warriors.": Scott Thomson, quoted in Brenda Breslauer et al., "Camden, N.J. Disbanded Its Police Force. Here's What Happened Next," NBC News, June 22, 2020, https://www.nbcnews.com/news/us-news/new-jersey-city -disbanded-its-police-force-here-s-what-n1231677.

102 "a department of . . . holistic, public-health-oriented approach": "Minneapolis City Council Members Taking First Step toward Disbanding City's Police Department," CBS News, June 26, 2020, https://www.cbsnews.com/news/minneapolis-city-council -members-taking-first-step-toward-disbanding-citys-police -department.

105 "Because abolition is . . . changing prevailing ideology.": Hanna Phifer, "For Angela Davis and Gina Dent, Abolition Is the Only Way," interview with Drs. Angela Y. Davis and Gina Dent, *Harper's Bazaar*, January 14, 2022, https://www.harpersbazaar .com/culture/art-books-music/a38746835/angela-davis-gina -dent-abolition-feminism-now-interview.

106 "People like me . . . efforts have failed.": Mariame Kaba, *We Do This 'Til We Free Us: Abolitionist Organizing and Transforming Justice* (Chicago: Haymarket Books, 2021), 56.

108 "everyone has access . . . and individuals thrive.": "Cultural Competence," Louisiana Department of Health, accessed February 18, 2022, https://ldh.la.gov/page/209.

109 "Change culture and . . . course of history.": Resmaa Menakem, *My Grandmother's Hands: Racialized Trauma and the Pathway to Mending Our Hearts and Bodies* (Las Vegas: Central Recovery, 2017), 245.

110 "racism, discrimination, and historical disenfranchisement": Rochelle P. Walensky, "Director's Commentary," Centers for Disease Control and Prevention, last updated October 25, 2021, https://www.cdc.gov/minorityhealth/racism-disparities/director-commentary.html.

111 "There are more . . . guns left over.": Christopher Ingraham, "There Are More Guns Than People in the United States, According to a New Study of Global Firearm Ownership," *Washington Post*, June 19, 2018, https://www.washingtonpost.com/news/wonk/wp/2018/06/19/there-are-more-guns-than-people-in-the-united-states-according-to-a-new-study-of-global-firearm-ownership.

113 "It's organising. It's . . . make the difference.": Lanre Bakare, "Angela Davis: 'We Knew That the Role of the Police Was to Protect White Supremacy,'" *Guardian* (US edition), June 15, 2020, https://www.theguardian.com/us-news/2020/jun/15/angela-davis-on-george-floyd-as-long-as-the-violence-of-racism-remains-no-one-is-safe.

114 "We can't arrest . . . of this problem.": Karen Brown, "Police Offering Drug Recovery Help: 'We Can't Arrest Our Way out of This Problem," NPR, February 8, 2020, https://www.npr.org/2020/02/08/802318886/police-offering-drug-recovery-help-we-can-t-arrest-our-way-out-of-this-problem.

115 "In a real . . . structure of reality.": "Honoring Reverend Dr. Martin Luther King, Jr.," Jewish Community Relations Council of Greater Washington, accessed January 24, 2023, https://www.jcouncil.org/page/honoring-reverend-dr-martin-luther-king-jr.

115 "make things right": "Restorative Justice," Minnesota Department of Corrections, accessed June 14, 2023, https://mn.gov/doc/victims/restorative-justice/.

118 "If we're really . . . services people need.": Jabali, "Do Cops Make Us Safe?"

118–119 "The best crime . . . have to worry.": Vikram Dodd, "Tackle Poverty and Inequality to Reduce Crime, Says Police Chief," *Guardian* (US edition), April 18, 2021, https://www.theguardian .com/uk-news/2021/apr/18/tackle-poverty-and-inequality-to -reduce-says-police-chief.

122 "The link between . . . to reading failure.": "Early Literacy Connection to Incarceration," Governor's Early Literacy Foundation, accessed January 24, 2023, https:// governorsfoundation.org/gelf-articles/early-literacy-connection -to-incarceration.

124–125 "community service allows . . . fair and just.": Carolyn Dallas et. al., A Five Year Look at Participation in the Time Dollar Youth Diversity Progress Report: 2004–2008, (Washington D.C.: TimeBanks Youth Court Intake Unit , 2008), 3.

128 "Now is the . . . or future year.": "Du Bois Quotes," W. E. B. Du Bois Center, accessed January 24, 2023, http://duboiscenter .library.umass.edu/du-bois-quotes.

129 "Freedom . . . is people . . . their own leaders.": Nita Clarke, "Diane Nash: Civil Rights Leader of My Generation," Network Lobby for Catholic Social Justice, February 25, 2022, https:// networklobby.org/22522dianenash.

131 "Racism is personal . . . power by institutions.": Tiffany Jewell, *This Book Is Anti-Racist* (Minneapolis: Frances Lincoln Children's Books, 2020), 30.

131 "Race, as we . . . of false consciousness.": Dr. Andrew Kiragu, "Moving beyond 'Race-Based' Medicine to 'Race-Conscious' Medicine," *Minnesota Spokesman-Recorder*, May 13, 2022, https://spokesman-recorder.com/2022/05/13/moving-beyond -race-based-medicine-to-race-conscious-medicine.

133 "Ultimately, restorative justice . . . accountability-based, and forward-looking.": Fania E. Davis, "What Is Restorative Justice?" Metro Detroit Restorative Justice Network, accessed June 14, 2023, https://metrodetroitrj.org/restorative-justice.

134 "The right of . . . to be seized.": U.S. Const., amend. IV.

134 "No person shall . . . without just compensation.": U.S. Const., amend. V.

135 "You have the . . . read to you?": "What Are Your Miranda Rights?" MirandaWarning.org, accessed January 24, 2023, http://www.mirandawarning.org/whatareyourmirandarights .html.

136 "In all criminal . . . for his defence.": U.S. Const., amend. VI.

136 "When people collectively . . . to effect change.": "The Spirituality of Nonviolence: The Soka Gakkai International Quarterly Interview with James Lawson," Satyagraha Foundation for Nonviolence Studies, December 8, 2016, http:// www.satyagrahafoundation.org/the-spirituality-of-nonviolence -the-soka-gakkai-international-quarterly-interview-with-james -lawson.

140 "I'm truly exhausted, . . . have no excuse.": Tiffany Crutcher quoted in "Four Years Later: Tiffany Crutcher Remembers the Life of Her Twin Brother, Terence," 2 News Oklahoma, September 16, 2020, https://www.kjrh.com/news/local-news /tiffany-crutcher-remembers-her-twin-brother-killed-four-years -ago-today.

SELECTED BIBLIOGRAPHY

"About the COPS Office." Office of Community Oriented Policing Services. Accessed February 6, 2022. https://cops.usdoj.gov/aboutcops.

"Arrests by Offense, Age, and Race." Office of Juvenile Justice and Delinquency Prevention. Accessed November 19, 2022. https://www .ojjdp.gov/ojstatbb/crime/ucr.asp?table_in=2&selYrs=2018&rdoGroups =1&rdoData=c.

Banaji, Mahzarin R., and Anthony G. Greenwald. *Blindspot: Hidden Biases of Good People.* New York: Bantam Books, 2016.

Berman, Mark. "Most Police Departments in America Are Small. That's Partly Why Changing Policing Is Difficult, Experts Say." *Washington Post*, May 8, 2021. https://www.washingtonpost.com/nation/2021/05/08/most-police -departments-america-are-small-thats-partly-why-changing-policing -is-difficult-experts-say.

"Black Wall Street in Tulsa, OK Destroyed on 6/1/1921." Library of Congress. Accessed January 18, 2023. https://guides.loc.gov/this -month-in-business-history/black-wall-street-destroyed.

Block, Melissa, and Elissa Nadworny. "Here's What's Become of a Historic All-Black Town in the Mississippi Delta." NPR, March 8, 2017. https://www .npr.org/2017/03/08/515814287/heres-whats-become-of-a-historic-all-black -town-in-the-mississippi-delta.

"Body Camera Laws by State 2023." World Population Review. Accessed December 14, 2022. https://worldpopulationreview.com/state-rankings /body-camera-laws-by-state.

Breslauer, Brenda, Kit Ramgopal, Kenzi Abou-Sabe, and Stephanie Gosk. "Camden, N.J. Disbanded Its Police Force. Here's What Happened Next." NBC News, June 22, 2020. https://www.nbcnews.com/news/us-news/new -jersey-city-disbanded-its-police-force-here-s-what-n1231677.

Bushey, Claire. "Defund the Police: How a Protest Slogan Triggered a Policy Debate." *Minneapolis/St. Paul Business Journal*, April 19, 2021. https://www .bizjournals.com/twincities/news/2021/04/19/defund-the-police-how-a -protest-slogan-triggered.html.

Camp, Jordan T., and Christina Heatherton. *Policing the Planet: Why the Policing Crisis Led to Black Lives Matter.* New York: Verso, 2016.

Cox, Megan. "The Relationships between Episodes of Parental Incarceration and Students' Psycho-Social and Educational Outcomes: An Analysis of Risk Factors." PhD dissertation, Temple University, 2009. http://hdl.handle.net/20.500.12613/1018.

Cunningham, Terrence M. "How Police and Communities Can Move Forward Together." American Bar Association, January 11, 2021. https://www.americanbar.org/groups/crsj/publications/human_rights_magazine_home/civil-rights-reimagining-policing/how-police-and-communities-can-move-forward-together/.

Davis, Angela. *Policing the Black Man: Arrest, Prosecution, and Imprisonment.* New York: Vintage Books, 2018.

Davis, Fania. *The Little Book of Race and Restorative Justice: Black Lives, Healing, and US Social Transformation.* New York: Good Books, 2019.

"De-Escalation Training: Safer Communities and Safer Law Enforcement Officers." Office of Justice Programs, September 6, 2022. https://www.ojp.gov/news/ojp-blogs/de-escalation-training-safer-communities-and-safer-law-enforcement-officers.

Dempsey, John S. *An Introduction to Policing.* Belmont, CA: Cengage, 2019.

DeSilver, Drew, Michael Lipka, and Dalia Fahmy. "10 Things We Know about Race and Policing in the U.S." Pew Research Center, June 3, 2020. https://www.pewresearch.org/fact-tank/2020/06/03/10-things-we-know-about-race-and-policing-in-the-u-s.

DeWolf, Thomas Norman, and Jodie Geddes. *The Little Book of Racial Healing: Coming to the Table for Truth-Telling, Liberation, and Transformation.* New York: Good Books, 2019.

Eberhardt, Jennifer Lynn. *Biased: The New Science of Race and Inequality.* London: William Heinemann, 2019.

Editors of Encyclopaedia Britannica. "Abraham Maslow." *Encyclopaedia Britannica.* Last updated December 30, 2022. https://www.britannica.com/biography/Abraham-H-Maslow.

———. "Black Code." *Encyclopaedia Britannica.* Last updated December 30, 2022. https://www.britannica.com/topic/black-code.

———. "Satyagraha." *Encyclopaedia Britannica.* Accessed January 18, 2023. https://www.britannica.com/topic/satyagraha-philosophy.

———. "Sir Robert Peel, 2nd Baronet Summary." *Encyclopedia Britannica*. Accessed November 26, 2022. https://www.britannica.com/summary /Robert-Peel.

Engel, Tagan. "Youth Leading Protests for Black Lives and Police Abolition." *Table Underground*, June 26, 2020. https://thetableunderground.com/the -table-underground/2020/6/25/teens-leading-protests-for-black-lives-amp -police-abolition.

"Eric Garner: Race." Esportfolios. Accessed December 13, 2022. https:// eportfolios.macaulay.cuny.edu/raceinnyc/eric-garner.

"Eyewitness: Confrontations for Justice." National Archives. Accessed January 18, 2023. https://www.archives.gov/exhibits/eyewitness/html.php ?section=2.

Fondren, Precious. "The 'Say Her Name' Movement Started for a Reason: We Forget Black Women Killed by Police." *Teen Vogue*, June 11, 2020. https://www.teenvogue.com/story/say-her-name-origin.

Franklin, V. P. *The Young Crusaders: The Untold Story of the Children and Teenagers Who Galvanized the Civil Rights Movement*. Boston: Beacon, 2021.

"Fruitvale Station and the Legacy of Oscar Grant." BET. Accessed December 19, 2022. https://www.bet.com/photo-gallery/cequhm/fruitvale -station-and-the-legacy-of-oscar-grant/6x9rue.

"George L. Kelling." Manhattan Institute. Accessed November 29, 2022. https://www.manhattan-institute.org/expert/george-l-kelling.

Glauser, Wendy. "Why Some Doctors Want to Defund the Police." *Canadian Medical Association Journal* 192, no. 48 (2020): E1644–E1645. https://doi.org/10.1503/cmaj.1095905.

Graham, Bryan Armen. "Donald Trump Blasts NFL Anthem Protestors: 'Get That Son of a Bitch off the Field.'" *Guardian* (US edition), September 23, 2017. https://www.theguardian.com/sport/2017/sep/22/donald-trump-nfl -national-anthem-protests.

Gray, Callan. "Lawmakers Suggest Police Residency Requirements, New Warrant Law as Session Nears End." KSTP. Last updated May 17, 2021. https://kstp.com/kstp-news/top-news/lawmakers-suggest-police -residency-requirements-new-warrant-law-as-session-nears-end.

Greene, Jack R. *The Encyclopedia of Police Science*. New York: Routledge, 2007.

"GuideStar Profile: Citywide Youth Coalition." GuideStar. Accessed November 12, 2022. https://www.guidestar.org/profile/06-1386638.

Harmon, Rick. "Timeline: The Selma-to-Montgomery Marches." *USA Today*. Last updated March 5, 2015. https://www.usatoday.com/story/news/nation/2015/03/05/black-history-bloody-sunday-timeline/24463923.

Harrell, Erika, and Elizabeth Davis. "Contacts between Police and the Public, 2018—Statistical Tables." Washington, DC, Bureau of Justice Statistics, 2020. https://bjs.ojp.gov/library/publications/contacts-between-police-and-public-2018-statistical-tables.

Harris, Paul. "Oakland Police: Controversial History Sets Tone for City's Discord." *Guardian* (US edition), October 26, 2011. https://www.theguardian.com/world/blog/2011/oct/26/oakland-police-department-black-community.

Hauck, Grace, and Mark Nichols. "Should Police Officers Be Required to Live in the Cities They Patrol? There's No Evidence It Matters." *USA Today*, June 13, 2020. https://www.usatoday.com/story/news/nation/2020/06/13/police-residency-data/5327640002.

"The History and Legacy of Eatonville, Florida's Pioneering African-American Town." James Madison Institute, December 6, 2017. https://jamesmadison.org/the-history-and-legacy-of-eatonville-floridas-pioneering-african-american-town-2.

History.com editors. "Angela Davis." History. Last updated January 26, 2021. https://www.history.com/topics/black-history/angela-davis.

———. "Eric Garner Dies in NYPD Chokehold." History, July 17, 2014. https://www.history.com/this-day-in-history/eric-garner-dies-nypd-chokehold.

———. "Tulsa Race Massacre." History. Last updated May 24, 2022. https://www.history.com/topics/roaring-twenties/tulsa-race-massacre.

Horace, Matthew, and Ron Harris. *The Black and the Blue: A Cop Reveals the Crimes, Racism, and Injustice in America's Law Enforcement*. New York: Hachette Books, 2018.

Horton, Jake. "How US Police Training Compares with the Rest of the World." BBC, May 18, 2021. https://www.bbc.com/news/world-us-canada-56834733.

Hrapsky, Chris. "Philando Castile Omnibus Bill Proposes $357 Million to End Systemic Racism." KARE 11. Last updated March 4, 2021. https://www.kare11.com/article/news/local/philando-castile/philando-castile-omnibus-bill-proposes-357-million-to-end-systemic-racism/89-ff2dcd6e-0aa7-441c-b345-c665b0a81114.

Hutchinson, Bill. "Derek Chauvin Wants to Go to Federal Prison, Even Though It Means He'll Do More Time." ABC News, December 21, 2021. https://abcnews.go.com/US/derek-chauvin-federal-prison-means-hell-time/story?id=81845835.

Ingraham, Christopher. "U.S. Spends Twice as Much on Law and Order as It Does on Cash Welfare, Data Show." *Washington Post*, June 4, 2020, https://www.washingtonpost.com/business/2020/06/04/us-spends-twice-much-law-order-it-does-social-welfare-data-show.

"The Issue." Reading Is Fundamental. Accessed December 17, 2022. https://www.rif.org/literacy-network/the-issue.

"James Q. Wilson." Pepperdine School of Public Policy. Accessed November 29, 2022. https://publicpolicy.pepperdine.edu/academics/faculty/james-wilson.

Jimenez, Omar. "3 Former Police Officers Charged in George Floyd's Death Reject Plea Deal." CNN. Last updated April 13, 2022. https://www.cnn.com/2022/04/12/us/george-floyd-officers-reject-plea-deal/index.html.

"July 28, 1917: Silent March Down Fifth Avenue." Zinn Education Project. Accessed December 13, 2022. https://www.zinnedproject.org/news/tdih/silent-march-nyc-naacp.

Kaba, Mariame. *We Do This 'Til We Free Us: Abolitionist Organizing and Transforming Justice*. Chicago: Haymarket Books, 2021.

"The King Philosophy—Nonviolence365." King Center. Accessed January 18, 2023. https://thekingcenter.org/about-tkc/the-king-philosophy.

Krogstad, Jens Manuel. "Latino Confidence in Local Police Lower Than among Whites." Pew Research Center, August 28, 2014. https://www.pewresearch.org/fact-tank/2014/08/28/latino-confidence-in-local-police-lower-than-among-whites.

Kummer, Jeffrey C., and Nicholas Bogel-Burroughs. "Last 2 Officers Involved in George Floyd's Death Are Sentenced to Prison." *New York Times*, July 27, 2022. https://www.nytimes.com/2022/07/27/us/george-floyd-j-alexander-kueng.html.

"Leadership in Police Organizations (LPO): Home." International Association of Chiefs of Police. Accessed December 13, 2022. https://www.theiacp.org/LPO.

LeCates, Rich. "Intelligence-Led Policing: Changing the Face of Crime Prevention." *Police Chief*, October 17, 2018. https://www.policechiefmagazine.org/changing-the-face-crime-prevention.

Lee, Jennifer. "Will Body Cameras Help End Police Violence?" American Civil Liberties Union of Washington, June 7, 2021. https://www.aclu-wa.org/story/%C2%A0will-body-cameras-help-end-police-violence%C2%A0.

Lepore, Jill. "The Invention of the Police." *New Yorker*, July 13, 2020. https://www.newyorker.com/magazine/2020/07/20/the-invention-of-the-police.

Lewis, Sukey, and Sandhya Dirks. "'On Our Watch' Litigation Reveals New Details in Police Shooting of Oscar Grant." *On Our Watch*. Produced by NPR, podcast, July 8, 2021. https://www.npr.org/2021/06/23/1009486885/on-our-watch-litigation-reveals-new-details-in-police-shooting-of-oscar-grant.

"Lynching in America: Confronting the Legacy of Racial Terror." 3rd ed. Equal Justice Initiative. Accessed January 18, 2023. https://lynchinginamerica.eji.org/report/.

Menakem, Resmaa. *My Grandmother's Hands: Racialized Trauma and the Pathway to Mending Our Hearts and Bodies*. Burlington, VT: Central Recovery, 2017.

Mu'min, Huda. "Ryan Coogler on 'Fruitvale Station.'" Interview by Ryan Coogler. *Washington Post*. Accessed January 5, 2022. https://www.washingtonpost.com/local/therootdc/ryan-coogler-on-fruitvale-station/2013/07/21/cd808d36-ee70-11e2-a1f9-ea873b7e0424_story.html.

Nash, Ashley. "Social Media & Social Justice since the Oscar Grant Shooting Video." Blavity, January 5, 2016. https://blavity.com/social-media-and-social-justice-since-oscar-grant/social-media-and-social-justice-since-oscar-grant?category1=opinion&category2=race-identity.

"National Alliance on Mental Illness: Home." National Alliance on Mental Illness. Accessed February 21, 2022. https://nami.org/home.

Neuhauser, Alan. "Cities Spend More and More on Police. Is It Working?" *US News*, July 7, 2017. https://www.usnews.com/news/national-news/articles/2017-07-07/cities-spend-more-and-more-on-police-is-it-working.

NewsOne staff. "136 Black Men and Boys Killed by Police." NewsOne, November 11, 2022. https://newsone.com/playlist/black-men-boys-who-were-killed-by-police/item/14.

Newton, Michael. *The Encyclopedia of American Law Enforcement*. New York: Facts on File, 2007.

Office of Community Oriented Policing Services. *Officer Health and Organizational Wellness. Emerging Issues and Recommendations*. Washington, DC: Office of Community Oriented Policing Services, 2018.

Orlando Sentinel. "Florida Teen Trayvon Martin Is Shot and Killed." History, February 26, 2012. https://www.history.com/this-day-in-history/florida-teen -trayvon-martin-is-shot-and-killed.

"The Police Badge—Origins and Meaning." Washington, DC Metropolitan Police Memorial and Museum. Accessed January 22, 2022. https://www .dcpolicememorial.org/the-police-badge-origins-and-meaning.

"Police Killings Can Harm Mental Health of Entire African American Community." Harvard T. H. Chan School of Public Health. Accessed February 19, 2022. https://www.hsph.harvard.edu/news/hsph-in-the -news/police-killings-can-harm-mental-health-of-entire-african-american -community.

"Police Killings of Unarmed Black Americans Affect Mental Health of Black Community." Penn Medicine News, June 21, 2018. https://www .pennmedicine.org/news/news-releases/2018/june/police-killings-of -unarmed-black-americans-affect-mental-health-of-black-community.

Porterfield, Carlie. "Police Officer Says He Falsely Charged Eric Garner after His Death." *Forbes*, October 26, 2021. https://www.forbes.com/sites /carlieporterfield/2021/10/26/police-officer-says-he-falsely-charged-eric -garner-after-his-death/?sh=692bac1f72d6.

"Procedural Justice." Justice Collaboratory, Yale Law School. Accessed December 13, 2022. https://law.yale.edu/justice-collaboratory/procedural- justice.

Purnell, Derecka. *Becoming Abolitionists: Police, Protests, and the Pursuit of Freedom*. New York: Astra House, 2021.

"Race Riots of the 1960s." Encyclopedia.com. Accessed January 18, 2023. https://www.encyclopedia.com/history/encyclopedias-almanacs -transcripts-and-maps/race-riots-1960s.

Rahr, Sue, and Stephen K. Rice. "From Warriors to Guardians: Recommitting American Police Culture to Democratic Ideals." Washington, DC: Bureau of Justice Statistics, 2015. https://www.ojp.gov/ncjrs/virtual -library/abstracts/warriors-guardians-recommitting-american-police -culture-democratic.

Reisig, Michael Dean, and Robert J. Kane. *The Oxford Handbook of Police and Policing.* Oxford: Oxford University Press, 2014.

"Report to the United Nations on Racial Disparities in the U.S. Criminal Justice System." Sentencing Project, April 19, 2018. https://www .sentencingproject.org/reports/report-to-the-united-nations-on -racial-disparities-in-the-u-s-criminal-justice-system.

Ritchie, Andrea J. *Invisible No More: Police Violence against Black Women and Women of Color.* Boston: Beacon, 2017.

Ritter, Mary Ellen, and Peter Diamond. "No-Knock Warrants in Minnesota: Explained." *Mpls.St.Paul*, February 11, 2022. https://mspmag.com/arts-and -culture/no-knock-warrants-in-minnesota-explained.

Roos, Dave. "The 1969 Raid That Killed Black Panther Leader Fred Hampton." History. Last updated February 3, 2021. https://www.history .com/news/black-panther-fred-hampton-killing.

Rothstein, Alexandra. "Join Us for a Community Resources and Gun Buyback Event in Minneapolis: Update on a Successful Event." Children's Minnesota. Accessed December 7, 2022. https://www.childrensmn.org/2022/10/20/join -us-community-resources-gun-buyback-event-minneapolis.

Santhanam, Laura. "Two-Thirds of Black Americans Don't Trust the Police to Treat Them Equally. Most White Americans Do." PBS, June 5, 2020. https:// www.pbs.org/newshour/politics/two-thirds-of-black-americans-dont-trust -the-police-to-treat-them-equally-most-white-americans-do.

"Seattle Police Department Manual: 8.100—De-Escalation." City of Seattle. Accessed November 30, 2022. https://www.seattle.gov/police-manual/title -8---use-of-force/8100---de-escalation.

Seattle Times editorial board. "Thank You, Sue Rahr, for Early Leadership on Police Reform." *Seattle Times.* Last updated May 10, 2021. https://www .seattletimes.com/opinion/editorials/gratitude-to-sue-rahr-an-early-leader -on-police-reform.

Schweikert, Jay. "Qualified Immunity." American Bar Association, December 17, 2020. https://www.americanbar.org/groups/public _education/publications/insights-on-law-and-society/volume-21 /issue-1/qualified-immunity.

Shrider, Emily A, Mellisa Kollar, Frances Chen, and Jessica Semega. "Income and Poverty in the United States: 2020." United States Census Bureau, September 14, 2021. https://www.census.gov/library /publications/2021/demo/p60-273.html.

Stamper, Norm. *To Protect and Serve: How to Fix America's Police.* New York: Nation Books, 2016.

Sterbenz, Christina. "How New York City Became Safe Again." Insider, December 2, 2014. https://www.businessinsider.com/criticism-for-giulianis -broken-windows-theory-2014-12.

"Stop-and-Frisk Data." New York Civil Liberties Union. Accessed December 19, 2022. https://www.nyclu.org/en/stop-and-frisk-data.

"A System Constructed to Fail Us All." Lakota People's Law Project, July 10, 2020. https://lakotalaw.org/news/2020-07-10/native-lives-matter-2020.

"10 Points about Race and Policing in the US." *Trust*, August 21, 2020. https://www.pewtrusts.org/en/trust/archive/summer-2020/10-points-about -race-and-policing-in-the-us.

"Terence Crutcher Foundation." Terence Crutcher Foundation. Accessed February 20, 2022. https://www.terencecrutcherfoundation.org.

Theoharis, Jeanne. "Martin Luther King Knew That Fighting Racism Meant Fighting Police Brutality." *Atlantic*, September 15, 2021. https://www .theatlantic.com/ideas/archive/2021/09/martin-luther-king-police -brutality/619090.

"Trayvon Martin Shooting Fast Facts." CNN. Last updated February 14, 2022. https://www.cnn.com/2013/06/05/us/trayvon-martin-shooting-fast -facts/index.html.

Treisman, Rachel. "Kentucky Law Limits Use of No-Knock Warrants, a Year after Breonna Taylor's Killing." NPR, April 9, 2021. https://www.npr.org /2021/04/09/985804591/kentucky-law-limits-use-of-no-knock-warrants-a -year-after-breonna-taylors-killin.

Trone Center for Justice and Equality. *Back to Business: How Hiring Formerly Incarcerated Job Seekers Benefits Your Company.* New York: American Civil Liberties Union, 2017.

Urofsky, Melvin I. "Jim Crow Law." *Encyclopaedia Britannica*. Accessed December 10, 2022. https://www.britannica.com/event/Jim-Crow-law.

US Department of Justice. *Federal Reports on Police Killings: Ferguson, Cleveland, Baltimore, and Chicago*. Brooklyn: Melville House, 2017.

Vedantam, Shankar, Chris Benderev, Tara Boyle, Renee Klahr, Maggie Penman, and Jennifer Schmidt. "How a Theory of Crime and Policing Was Born, and Went Terribly Wrong." NPR, November 1, 2016. https://www.npr .org/2016/11/01/500104506/broken-windows-policing-and-the-origins-of -stop-and-frisk-and-how-it-went-wrong.

Vitale, Alex S. *The End of Policing*. New York: Verso, 2021.

Westervelt, Eric. "Mental Health and Police Violence: How Crisis Intervention Teams Are Failing." NPR, September 18, 2020. https://www .npr.org/2020/09/18/913229469/mental-health-and-police-violence-how -crisis-intervention-teams-are-failing.

Wiltz, Teresa. "'A Pileup of Inequities': Why People of Color Are Hit Hardest by Homelessness." Stateline, March 29, 2019. https://www.pewtrusts .org/en/research-and-analysis/blogs/stateline/2019/03/29/a-pileup-of -inequities-why-people-of-color-are-hit-hardest-by-homelessness.

Wyllie, Doug. "11 Inspirational Quotes to Boost Police Morale in Trying Times." *Police Magazine*, April 17, 2020. https://www.policemag.com /551308/11-inspirational-quotes-to-boost-police-morale-in-trying-times.

Yancey-Bragg, N'dea. "Push to Disband Minneapolis Police Fails Despite Calls for Reform after George Floyd's Death." *USA Today*. Last updated November 3, 2021. https://www.usatoday.com/story/news/nation/2021 /11/02/minneapolis-police-proposal-dismantle-department-fails /8564868002.

FURTHER INFORMATION

Books

Alexander, Michelle. *The New Jim Crow: Mass Incarceration in the Age of Colorblindness*. 10th ed. New York: New Press, 2020.

Braun, Eric. *The Civil Rights Movement*. Minneapolis: Lerner Publications, 2019.

———. *Taking Action for Civil and Political Rights*. Minneapolis: Lerner Publications, 2017.

Magoon, Kekla. *Revolution in Our Time: The Black Panther Party's Promise to the People*. Somerville, MA: Candlewick, 2021.

Smith, Elliott, and Cicely Lewis. *Slavery and Reconstruction: The Struggle for Black Civil Rights*. Minneapolis: Lerner Publications, 2022.

Tyner, Artika R. *Black Lives Matter: From Hashtag to the Streets*. Minneapolis: Lerner Publications, 2021.

Wilkerson, Isabel. *Caste: The Origins of Our Discontents*. New York: Random House, 2020.

Documentaries

DuVernay, Ava. *13th*. Oakland: Forward Movement/Kandoo Films, 2016.

Nelson, Stanley. *Black Panthers: Vanguard of the Revolution*. Arlington, VA: PBS Distribution, 2016.

Policing the Police. YouTube video, 53:16. Posted by *Frontline* PBS. https://www.youtube.com/watch?v=2_8vTl6D940.

Websites

Community Oriented Policing Services Program
https://cops.usdoj.gov/communitypartnerships
The site provides resources for building partnerships between law enforcement and communities.

Policing in America
https://eji.org/issues/policing-in-america/
Explore the history of policing in the United States.

Strategies for Youth
    https://strategiesforyouth.org/
    The site seeks to support interactions between police officers and
    youth.

Street Law
    https://www.streetlaw.org/articles/teaching-law-as-a-life-skill-how
    -street-law-empowers-vulnerable
    Gain an understanding and knowledge about your legal rights.

Twenty-First-Century Policing
    https://cops.usdoj.gov/RIC/Publications/cops-p341-pub.pdf
    Explore the best practices in policing to reduce crime and build public
    trust in this US Department of Justice publication, *The President's Task
    Force on 21st Century Policing*.

Working Group on Police-Involved Deadly Force Encounters
    https://dps.mn.gov/divisions/co/working-group/Pages/default.aspx
    The site has resources and recommendations to address and reduce
    officer-involved shootings.

INDEX

ABOUT THE AUTHOR

Dr. Artika Tyner is a passionate educator, award-winning author, civil rights attorney, sought-after speaker, and advocate for justice. She lives in Saint Paul, Minnesota, and is the founder of the Planting People Growing Justice Leadership Institute, a national program that focuses on promoting reading and increasing diversity in books to dismantle the pipeline to prison. This is of critical importance due to the connection between illiteracy and future incarceration and the overrepresentation of communities of color in the criminal justice system. Its goal is to create new pipelines to success by improving literacy rates and inspiring the next generation of leaders.

PHOTO ACKNOWLEDGMENTS

Image credits: Tim Evans/Bloomberg/Getty Images, p. 9; Luis Sinco/Los Angeles Times/Getty Images, p. 10; AP Photo/Court TV, p. 11; Independent Picture Service, p. 15, 32, 33, 53, 54, 55, 83, 96, 119; Kean Collection/Getty Images, p. 18; Bettmann/Getty Images, p. 19, 26, 36; Wikimedia Commons PD, p. 21; FPG/Hulton Archive/Getty Images, p. 28; AP Photo/Barry Thumma, p. 31; Enigma/Alamy, p. 35; Matthew J. Lee/The Boston Globe/Getty Images, p. 34; Library of Congress, p. 38, 42; Frank Rockstroh/Michael Ochs Archives/Getty Images, p. 41; AP Photo, p. 44; © Ted Streshinsky/CORBIS/Getty Images, p. 47; AP Photo/Daniel Gluskoter, p. 56; Alexi Rosenfeld/Getty Images, p. 59; Stephen Maturen/Getty Images, p. 60; Justin Sullivan/Getty Images, p.64; Carlos Avila Gonzalez/The San Francisco Chronicle/Getty Images (left), p. 67; AP Photo/Carlos Osorio (center), p. 67; Anacleto Rapping/Los Angeles Times/Getty Images (right), p. 67; Mark Bonifacio/New York Daily News/Tribune News Service/Getty Images, p. 69; © Stan Carroll/The Commercial Appeal/ZUMAPRESS.com/Alamy, p. 70; Jerod Harris/Getty Images, p. 75; Ricky Carioti/ The Washington Post/Getty Images, p. 87; Spencer Platt/Getty Images, p. 76; Circa Images/GHI/Universal History Archive/Universal Images Group/Getty Images, p. 78; UPI/Alamy, p. 82; Stephen Maturen/Getty Images, p. 89; VDB Photos/Shutterstock, p. 91; Patrick Whittemore/MediaNews Group/Boston Herald/Getty Images, p. 93; Jerry Holt/Star Tribune/Getty Images, p. 97; © Neal Skorpen, p. 98; Bastiaan Slabbers/NurPhoto/Getty Images, p. 101; Allison C Bailey/Shutterstock, p. 104; Courtesy of the University of Wisconsin - Madison, p. 71; Courtesy of Oregon State University, p. 105; Greg Nash-Pool/Getty Images, p. 110; Liz Hafalia/The San Francisco Chronicle via Getty Images, p. 112; Craig F. Walker/The Boston Globe/Getty Images, p. 114; ShadeDesign/Shutterstock, p. 121; Johnny Nunez/WireImage/Getty Images, p. 122; Rick Loomis/Los Angeles Times/Getty Images, p.126; Stephen Maturen/Getty Images, p. 128; Genaro Molina/Los Angeles Times/Getty Images, p. 130; Paul Kuroda/San Francisco Chronicle/Getty Images, p. 132; AP Photo/Sean McKeag/The Citizens' Voice, p. 137. Design elements: Arcady/Shutterstock; Yurlick/Shutterstock.